THE CHURCH IN THE ANCIENT WORLD

THE CHURCH IN THE ANCIENT WORLD

By

L. E. ELLIOTT-BINNS, D.D.

LONDON
JOHN HERITAGE
THE UNICORN PRESS

NEW YORK

First published 1938
All rights reserved

Made in Great Britain. Printed by SHERRATT & HUGHES, at the St. Ann's Press, Manchester.

TO THE MEMORY OF
HENRY MELVILL GWATKIN
UNDER WHOSE GUIDANCE
I BEGAN THE SERIOUS STUDY
OF THE CHURCH IN THE ANCIENT WORLD

PREFACE

This small volume does not profess to give, even in outline, a complete history of the Church in the first three centuries of the Christian era. What I have written has been conditioned strictly by the title of the series as a whole, and is intended to lead up to the culminating chapter in which I have tried to show how the Church opposed its own challenge to that of the world into which it came.

With some of the questions, here treated only superficially, I hope to deal more fully in a work on the beginnings of Western Christianity, upon which I have been engaged for some years.

L. E. E.-B.

CONTENTS

CHAPTER	PAGE
PREFACE	7
I. THE WORLD INTO WHICH THE CHURCH CAME	11
II. THE FIRST AGES OF THE CHURCH	32
III. THE STRUGGLE WITH THE EMPIRE	52
IV. THE STRUGGLE WITH HERESY AND SCHISM	77
V. THE ORGANISATION OF THE CHURCH	101
VI. THE GROWTH OF DOGMA	121
VII. THE CHURCH'S ACHIEVEMENT	141
INDEX	169

CHAPTER I

THE WORLD INTO WHICH THE CHURCH CAME

THE rise and progress of the Christian Church in the Ancient World constitutes one of the most dramatic series of events in the whole of history. But if it has the nature of a drama, that drama must not be regarded as complete and finished; Early Church history forms no period in the narrow sense of the word, for it is still going on. It is not something past and dead, but part of the present in which we ourselves are living; in fact, reverting to the figure of a drama, we must not be content, as we contemplate it, to look upon ourselves as mere spectators sitting in the stalls, but rather as actors waiting to take our own place on the stage. The Church on earth lives on, though its members may pass from the scene, just as a mighty forest persists through season after season, though the leaves may fall from the trees and the trees themselves decay and give place to others.

In the fact that our story is concerned not merely with events which happened and were forgotten, but with living issues, lies its supreme interest and importance. Moreover, it is only when so regarded that it becomes really available for ourselves. In order to penetrate beneath the husk of mere outward events we must be willing to see life as the early Christians saw it; must attempt to share their pains and perplexities as well as their joys and triumphs—to wander with Justin on the seashore and face with Blandina the horrors of the amphitheatre. So we begin our drama with a description of the background against which the opening act was played—the world in which the Church arose. This description has a double importance, for not only is the knowledge of it essential to a grasp of the real meaning of the Church's triumph, but also because it reveals the environment in which the men and women were trained and educated from whom the Church was to draw its first members.

The first point to be observed is the extent to which the world was under a single rule. The Roman eagle was supreme, in the words of Sohm, the German lawyer and historian, " not only on the Rhine, but on the Danube, the Euphrates, the Nile, at the foot of the Atlas Mountains and of the Pyrenees ". With only slight exceptions early Christianity was to spread within the limits of the empire which had its seat at Rome. This empire, unlike the still vaster empire of which we are members, was not worldwide and ' farflung '; it was, indeed, a very compact affair, everywhere continuous and stretched around the Mediterranean, which in the first few centuries of our era could fairly be described as a Roman lake. Towards the north and the east, it is true, there were dangerous extensions, but a wise moderation allowed the renunciation of further ambitions in these directions. Behind the well-guarded frontier—that proud Roman frontier which was nothing more than a fortified road—there was good order and peace.

This settled state of affairs was of only recent birth when Christ came, for it followed a century or so of anarchy and civil strife in which rival generals and their armies had fought for the control of the Republic. A long series of struggles had been ended at last when Augustus overcame the revolutionary elements by force of arms and, in the final contest with Antony and Cleopatra, saved the West from separation from the East or, as an alternative, from political subjection. Augustus became the first of the long line of Roman emperors, but as he preferred to disguise his actual power many of the older republican forms, which had proved so inadequate a check on the ambition of military leaders, were still retained. Augustus was a lover of peace, and it was fitting that his greatest contribution to the welfare of the empire was not gained on the field of battle, but lay in the foundation of a new administrative system; a system which proved strong enough to survive even the vagaries of Nero. Under him and his successors trade and commerce expanded rapidly, and since it was left largely to non-Romans and freedmen whole swarms of enterprising Orientals quickly flooded the West; a circumstance which had repercussions in other departments than the commercial. The vast system of roads continually extended and carefully repaired — such work was a useful method of employing the legionaries in times of peace—helped the spread of trade and of new ideas. Travel was, on the whole, safe, though the unprotected wayfarer might encounter hazards in the remoter districts. If travel was easy by land it was equally easy by sea, since the energy of Pompey, in the previous generation, had swept the pirates from the Eastern Mediterranean.

Within the vast ring of the Empire many kingdoms and provinces were included, the fruit of the conquering arms of the Roman legions. Such kingdoms and provinces were allowed to retain much of their old forms of government—there was no attempt to impose one uniform system. But in every province, towns, or colonies, each modelled on Rome, quickly sprang up as centres of power and influence. The significance of these cities and of the older municipalities has been well brought out by B. W. Henderson:

"No one," he writes, "can realise the history of the Roman Empire or the significance of the Roman civilisation for every succeeding age who does not always bear in mind that the town, with its local self-government and keen vivid life, was the foundation upon which the whole Roman culture and liberty were firmly based. One thousand years of vigorous civic life was Rome's contribution to European history."[1]

For the Christian Church the town was also significant, and the importance of the cities of Asia Minor in

[1] *The Life and Principate of the Emperor Hadrian*, p. 180. The importance of the towns began to diminish after the middle of the third century: see Rostovtzeff *Social and Economic History of the Roman Empire*, ch. ix–xi.

particular can hardly be exaggerated for the first two centuries of the history of the Church.

Peace and stability thus reigned within the Empire with increasing trade and its accompaniment of growing luxury. But beyond the frontiers there was ever present danger. Indeed from the days when Marius, by heroic exertions, drove back the Cimbri, the Roman world, in spite of frequent sallies across the borders along which her sentries kept their ceaseless vigil, was really in a state of siege. From time to time trouble would flare up, and after a crisis be crushed out; but the threat was ever there. So the armies of the Empire were massed on the frontiers where they came to form permanent settlements and to add to the mixture of races.

Such very briefly was the political situation in the era when the Church was growing up within the Empire. Perhaps even more important were the social conditions which must now receive attention.

When Bishop Lightfoot came to prepare the second edition of his famous *Apostolic Fathers* he began with a quotation from Goethe to the effect that the literature which survives from any particular epoch is only a fragment of what was actually written in it. This is true of the Christian literature of the Sub-Apostolic Age, to which Lightfoot applied it; but it is almost equally true of literature in general during the whole of the first few centuries of our era. The great writers, upon whom historians relied in the past for their estimate of the social and moral condition of the Roman people, were restricted in the area of their observations as well as limited in time. They belong to the first and early second century and are interested only in the doings of certain wealthy and prominent circles in the capital of the Empire. It had, of course, always been known, from the writings of Pliny the Younger, if nowhere else, that the picture which they painted was too dark to be applied universally, and that in the country and the smaller towns things were not nearly so corrupt. The recent intensive study of the numerous inscriptions which have been preserved shows quite clearly, even when allowance has been made for conventional phraseology, that the Roman people were much sounder at heart and had a much fuller appreciation of the old Roman virtues and the religious system upon which they rested than had previously been supposed. None the less conditions were truly grave. The price paid for peace and stability, now that it had come at last, had been grievous; to the bloodshed of the numerous wars must be added the sufferings of the countless multitudes who formed the base upon which the whole structure of society was erected. Those for whom that structure seemed to exist were quite unworthy of the cost of preserving it, for the luxury and vice of the aristocracy were matched by the brutality and greed of the populace. Rome, in winning the world, had lost her own soul. The old virtues, devotion to country, stern discipline, respect for constituted authority, even respect for self, had all been weakened. Life had lost its simplicity, and honour and fortitude had gone with it. The old dignity and self-control in which the Roman had prided himself above all else had vanished save in the few, and it was noticeable that the better classes were most prone to exhibitions of passion and loss of nerve.

The age, as revealed in the doings and sayings of the wealthy, was an artificial one. The ordinary, natural pleasures of life had lost their edge for men who commanded vast resources and had often exhausted them before reaching manhood; something more exciting was demanded. The inevitable result was swift degeneration of morals and the growth of unnatural vice. The best stock of the nation had by this time almost completely disappeared, killed off in warfare against public enemies abroad and in civil strife and proscriptions at home.[1] With their passing went also the old splendid family life of the Romans; divorces were frequent, and unwanted children were quietly disposed of or exposed. The bringing up of children, once the proud task of the parents themselves, was now left to slaves; and if Quintilian is to be believed, this was an advantage, for he affirms that in many households the influence of the parents was more harmful than that of the slaves.

Slaves probably formed something like half the population of the Empire. Some of them were engaged in domestic service; others worked in gangs on the great

---

[1] After the Peloponnesian War Isocrates noted that the same thing had happened at Athens. The old families had been wiped out and the roll of citizens was full of the names of aliens 'from all sorts of places' (*De Pace*, 86–89).

plantations. The plantation system with its cruelties and horrors was a feature of the West; in the East the slave had a much easier lot, as he had indeed in a household in the West. Slavery, however, was not necessarily a permanent condition, and many slaves succeeded in acquiring their freedom; so many, in fact, that the freedman played an important part in the history of Rome and the Empire.

Economically the age was one of growing strain. The immense sums frittered away in vulgar ostentation were often raised at the expense of more needful and more profitable expenditure; and so capital was wasted and land went out of cultivation. But the whole method of land cultivation with its immense plantations worked by slaves was unhealthy. It dispossessed the small farmer and peasant and drove them into the towns where they swelled the mass of unemployed and paupers. Trade was despised by the aristocrat and thus became the chosen sphere of the freedman and the alien. These latter in consequence acquired vast wealth and the influence which sooner or later follows its possession.

The swarms of unemployed had somehow to be fed and amused lest they should provoke dangerous uproars and inconvenient strife; so " bread and free amusements " became their motto. In any case the problem of the organisation of leisure, which is only now becoming acute in modern times with the progress of invention, was one which had already to be faced in those rich southern lands with their bounteous climate. And so at least twice in each week there were public spectacles, games, and shows of one kind or another. By them the lust for blood and the taste for indecency were cultivated and encouraged. Thus human life and virtue came to be assessed at a very low price by the Roman mob. And the mobs of other cities were not far behind them, though their opportunities were not so great. The wealthy amused themselves in their own way and fought stoutly against the tedium of life. Travel was easy and popular, and they had their country villas where some chance of a healthier atmosphere, physically and morally, was theirs.

When all allowance has been made for partiality and exaggeration the state of the Roman people with its brutal selfishness, its shameless immorality, and its vulgar ostentation was decidedly unpleasing. In an atmosphere such as that described above—and if the people of Rome have been most prominent in it they were but typical of the Empire—the Gospel had to make its way, and simple Christian souls to live out their lives. What made it still harder was the fact that the whole social system was intertwined with pagan religious observances, polytheism permeated it as in present-day India. Even the public spectacles had a religious basis, whilst public and private banquets, and trade itself, demanded contact with the popular deities; whilst the army, the civil service, and the teaching profession involved conformity of a definite kind. There was also the position of the Christian slave employed by a heathen master to be considered. These matters formed a very grave problem for the first generations of Christians, and their abstention from social life earned for them the reputation of being haters of mankind. Later they became less strict, as the world entered into the Church and familiarity seemed to rob Paganism of its perils. At last Christians were to be found in almost all professions, some even accepted office as pagan priests, and the games and theatrical shows did not lack their presence.

One feature of the social life of the times was the existence of large numbers of clubs or associations. Not a great deal is said about them in the literature which has survived, but from the inscriptions it is possible to realise the important part which they played in the life of the people. Under the Republic there had been no objection to the formation of such bodies, any group of citizens might start one; but under Julius restrictions began to be imposed, and under the Empire there was very careful supervision. The majority of such associations were under religious patronage, in this they resembled the guilds of the Middle Ages, and like them one of the chief objects was the provision of due funeral rites for the members. Some were actually formed as religious societies. The newly founded Christian congregations came under the heading of these societies, though it was long before they succeeded in getting official recognition, with the consequent legal protection and rights which this involved. One function of such bodies was to provide an outlet for the organising abilities of individuals who were in general debarred from taking any part in politics after the incorporation of the city-states in the world-wide Empire. This function was very similar to that of the Nonconformist societies in England before the extension of the franchise.

We turn now to view the ancient world from the standpoint of culture. At first sight it would seem that within the framework of the single vast political system a single cultural system, that with which conquered Greece had led captive its conquerors, alone prevailed. And in the main such an impression would be a just one, though it is important to remember that a number of peoples and cultures, although strongly influenced, remained unabsorbed. Such were the Celts of Gaul and Britain, the Aramaic-speaking peoples of Syria, the Copts of Egypt, and the dwellers in the remoter parts of Asia Minor. In some of these districts Christianity tended to spread, not as elsewhere among the lower classes, but among the educated who knew a little Greek.[1] In fact it was the Christian Church and not the Roman Government which in parts of Asia Minor finally overcame the primitive native language and substituted Greek. But if the Roman world was not completely Greek in culture the language and philosophy of the Greeks were predominant. This enabled men to overleap those national barriers which military

---

[1] This was probably not the case in Britain, where Christianity seems to have spread only among the poorer classes in the towns and among "considerable numbers whose degree of romanisation was very small; people whose names and speech and manners, in spite of three centuries of Roman government, were still prevailingly Celtic." (Collingwood & Myres, *Roman Britain*, p. 272.)

conquest and political reorganisation had already made less definite. Culture formed that mental necessity which is almost the modern equivalent for fate, and by it the many peoples of the Empire were compelled, consciously or otherwise, to look at life and to judge of its problems from a certain fixed point of view. Furthermore it has to be remembered that Hellenic mythology permeated ancient literature and art.

By the first century of the Christian era, however, Greek culture, which the arms of Alexander the Great had carried far into Asia, was past its noontide. It had "failed to master the intractable soul of the Orient", and in the struggle had itself been greatly modified and changed. None the less it was still a quickening force making life, as well as literature and art, richer and more beautiful by its influence. In spite of some modification it still tended to be exclusive and scornful of other cultures, and the history of European civilisation, and of the Church in particular, might have been very different if Latin had been known in the East as Greek was known in the West.[1]

By this time Latin culture was also verging towards its decline. When the Church set out to win the world for Christ the Augustan Age was already past, and the giants who had adorned it were to find no equal successors. In one art alone was superiority to be mani-

---

[1] The Greeks were surprisingly bad linguists. Herodotus knew no Egyptian or Persian and Plutarch's knowledge of Latin was imperfect. No wonder that anyone who was possessed of two languages excited comment (cf. Thucydides viii, 85). See further T. R. Glover, *From Pericles to Philip*, p. 224.

fested—that of architecture. But it is an open question whether the mania for erecting vast buildings, which persisted into the Age of Constantine, was really a healthy phenomenon. Certainly the rivalry of certain of the municipalities involved them deeply in debt; as later a similar competition was to embarrass the finances of the medieval abbeys. But it may be that to vie with one's neighbours in architectural achievement is less reprehensible than to join them in an endless armaments race.

In the sphere of religion as in those of culture and politics there was also an attempt, which will be considered below, to provide a single, all-inclusive system—the worship of Rome as linked with or incarnate in the reigning Emperor.

Roman religion in early times had been very simple. In each household the head of the family had performed the necessary offices in honour of the recognised deities and had striven to inculcate those typical Roman virtues which were based upon it. To a later mind the whole thing may seem rather dull and quite lacking in spirituality; but within its limits it was amazingly effective. The more public religion followed much the same lines; the great object was to gain or retain the favour of the gods by the exact performance of the stated ritual. Upon this depended, so it was held, the safety and prosperity of the State. Thus magic and not religion was its real essence. Augustus himself strove valiantly to revive the traditional religion which by his day had no longer much hold on the minds of the more educated, and built new temples to adorn and safeguard the new Empire of which he was likewise the founder.

But if scepticism was widespread among the ruling classes they did not neglect outward conformity. Why should they when such was hardly considered a sign of religious belief, but rather of political loyalty? (This is a point which needs to be borne in mind in connexion with the Persecution of the Christians.) Unbelief, as always, was accompanied by gross superstition. Ghosts and demons haunted men's lives, bringing disease and misfortune; against their attacks it was necessary to invoke the aid of magic arts and those who practised them. From time to time decrees were issued ordering the expulsion of such professors from Italy, together with astrologers and even philosophers. But this action was taken, not because the ruling emperor disapproved of the practices as such, but because their aid was sought in plots against his person and office. Magic and treason had become almost synonymous terms.

Whilst the peasants and the common people held a traditional faith of an animistic kind, worshipping the gods of the farm and field, the hearth and home, the more sophisticated supplemented or displaced them by imported deities of a more definite character. Contact with Greek religion and the numerous cults of the East in itself was bound to produce an effect. The similarity between the official deities of the Latins and the Greeks was sufficient to lead to their identification; just as in an earlier age the invading Greeks themselves had, not without syncretism and modification, added their own deities, mostly of a male kind, to the worship of the mother goddess which they found established in the conquered territories. Religion in Greece as in Italy had by this time become a matter of the observance of an outward ritual whose underlying myths were rejected by the cultivated.

The inflow of Eastern cults was a different matter. They were brought back by Roman citizens who had served in the wars or been administrators in the East—the two generally went together—or introduced by the swarms of Orientals who came to the West. Precedent could be found in the bringing of the Great Mother from Phrygia in 205 B.C. after the Sibylline Books had been consulted. The process thus inaugurated went on, and the cults of Syrian and Egyptian deities were quickly added until Rome, in the words of Gibbon, "became the common temple of her subjects, and the freedom of the city was bestowed on all the gods".

In the land of their origin these various cults were practised with greater freedom than in Rome, where some kind of supervision was exercised and the most indecent features were curtailed. No Roman was allowed to act as priest of the Great Mother. Her cult was exceedingly ancient and widespread, and in various guises underlay many of the native religions. In Egypt the worship of Isis and Serapis attracted many, as it did indeed in the West after the first feeling of abhorrence had been overcome.

At one time it used to be thought that Christianity had a serious rival in the cult of Mithras. This ancient deity, a god of light who had come to be identified with the sun, became known in the Empire shortly before the Christian era; possibly, as one of the fruits of Pompey's drive against the Cilician pirates. His worship spread rapidly, but only within a limited area. Soldiers were attracted by the courage and aggressiveness of the god, and merchants and slaves were numbered among his votaries. Some of the emperors and a number of select circles also took up the cult, but it was never a possible substitute for Christianity as a universal religion.[1] Perhaps the fact that women were excluded may explain its want of greater success. As in the case of other rivals of the Gospel certain common features, possibly due to borrowing on the one side or the other, can be discovered.

Alongside religions of a more open and established kind, and often in conjunction with them, went the mysteries. Many of them perhaps had been carried on in secret from remote ages and forgotten civilisations, now they took their place in the religious life of the world. In spite of the variety of their sources, the mysteries had much in common; salvation and immortality were offered to those partaking in certain rites. These rites were usually connected with the story of some divine or quasi-divine being, to whom, as the crowning-point, the initiate was to be united. The claims of these cults were such as to make a general

---

[1] See A. D. Nock in *Journal of Roman Studies*, xxvii, p. 113.

appeal, and the fact that no class was excluded added to their attractiveness. The rites themselves produced religious ecstasy and were often of a frenzied nature. The higher types, however, demanded in those who wished to be initiated, especially into the more advanced stages of the cult, a good deal of courage and self-control, for severe tests had to be undergone. For many the mysteries must have represented a distinct achievement in the religious, and perhaps in the moral, life; and if their extravagant promises were not completely fulfilled they whetted the appetite for something better. The god of the Christians was also a Saviour.

For the higher minds philosophies of various brands still had their attraction. In Rome and Italy the Stoics were to prove most influential; but they made but little appeal to the crowd, they were too aloof and cold, too entirely lacking in the means of arousing religious enthusiasm and sentiment, which indeed they would have condemned. In Alexandria Stoicism had taken on a different colour under the influence of the followers of Pythagoras and of Plato. There too, as elsewhere, Neo-Platonism flourished. This philosophy owed much indeed to Plato, much also to Oriental beliefs and attitudes. It was mystical in tone, with an immense emphasis on the littleness of man and the magnitude of God. But like Stoicism it made but small appeal to the masses; the vision of God and final absorption in the divine essence they hoped to attain through the mysteries. The great name among Neo-Platonists, towards the end of our period, was Plotinus.

Most of the philosophical systems were tending to become dull and dreary as they became more and more elaborate and involved. One striking exception was the school of the Cynics. Teachers of this school descended into the market-place and taught all who would listen to them. No doubt with their insistence on the supremacy of virtue and of man's ability to live the good life they aroused in many the desire for moral attainment and prepared the way for the message of the Church. The Cynic teachers wandered about from place to place and so were like not only the Jewish and Christian missionary but the wandering sophist of the days of Socrates. In his day those who desired so to wander had to restrict themselves very severely or else to sacrifice civic loyalty in order to gain mobility. Now men were members of a single empire and could wander far and wide without traversing its borders.

The general philosophical outlook of the times, whether explicit or implied, was one of fatalism. This fatalism was connected closely in many minds with the movements of the stars upon which the fortunes of states and individuals alike were thought to depend. Hence the importance of astrology, and its pretended power to foretell the future and to announce the happiness or otherwise of any special hour for undertaking new enterprises.

In matters of religion the Roman Government was distinctly tolerant; the Pantheon was always open to receive fresh candidates, so long as no political dangers were likely to follow their recognition, as in the case of the Druids and their gods. But Roman religion, even when reinforced by diverse Oriental cults, was plainly incapable of meeting the needs of the people. The very introduction of such cults sapped the official faith and proclaimed its insufficiency. But they did at least keep alive the religious instinct of the individual and provide a religion which, since the votary was free to accept or reject it, could be called personal. They even helped to raise the moral ideas of some; but anything like moral uplift on a large scale was obviously beyond their power.

To weld it together the Empire, as Augustus soon foresaw, needed the help of a single religion. And so the cult of Rome and the Emperor was encouraged. The idea of Emperor-worship arose in the East, where the distinction between gods and men was not so nice as in the West. There the cult of the ruler, sometimes as the incarnation of the god, had long been practised; even Alexander the Great had been worshipped in his lifetime. In a similar way temples were erected to Augustus in Asia Minor. We have no reason for supposing that he was anxious to receive such homage, but he did not forbid it; politically there was much in its favour. In the West, however, the Emperor was not for some time regarded as a god until after his death; hence the facetious remark of the dying Vespasian: "I think that I am about to become a god." But the worship of the living Emperor was not long in following.

Emperor-worship was much more active in the

provinces, where it was most useful, than in Rome and Italy, and an elaborate organisation was established to maintain it. In course of time it came to be treated less and less seriously, and by the third century the public games which marked the annual festivals had become their most prominent feature. In any case, it was an exercise of the community, not of the individual, and could not arouse religious feeling. None the less the cult had its share in preparing for Christianity, for it gave an example of a religion as widespread as the Empire itself, and, since it was often combined with local cults, helped to co-ordinate the various competing religions.

In this sketch of the religious beliefs of the Empire, and especially of those of Rome itself, towards which they all tended to progress, I have said nothing so far of that Jewish faith out of which Christianity itself was to arise. The omission is deliberate as Judaism and the part it played can best be studied in the following chapter when we consider the life of the first generations of Christians.

Such, then, was the religious state of the Empire, and into this welter of faiths and philosophies Christianity had to make its way. What were its prospects, and how would it deal with its rivals? The disciples of other religions, save the stubborn Jews, were tolerant and not at all averse to welcoming an additional object of worship. A new god was as interesting as a new author or a novel fashion. But the God of the Christians would hear of no rival, and a religion which taught that no man can serve two masters was obviously not going to take its place, on easy terms, in any syncretic congeries of faiths. So there must be a struggle, a desperate fight for mastery, and in that struggle the narrow exclusiveness which was characteristic of Christianity helped not a little towards its final triumph; for exclusiveness has an attractive power, and the fear and hatred of Paganism kept the Church, especially in the earliest days, reasonably free from compromising accretions.

CHAPTER II

THE FIRST AGES OF THE CHURCH

THE most important development which took place in the first ages of Christianity was its gradual emancipation from the Jewish Church in which it had originated. This was a necessary step, for the husk of Judaism had to be broken if the universal mission of Christianity was to be realised. Before going on to describe the sequence of this development, however, it will be useful to take note of the various facilities which the Jewish people provided for the spread and triumph of the Church.

In the first place it is to be noted that they had been dispersed, by war and commerce, over the greater part of the Roman world. Their numbers were naturally greatest in Syria and the East; but elsewhere, even in the West, they had numerous centres. Wherever they went considerable influence came their way, and the instinct for trade led them to settle almost entirely in cities, where access to the largest number of people was possible. The simple method by which a synagogue could be formed led to their establishment wherever a few Jewish people capable of meeting together could be found; and it was to the synagogue first that the Christian missionary would naturally go. Judaism itself was a missionary religion with a skilled and energetic propaganda in process. Thus the Jews of the Dispersion not only provided a base from which the Christians could work, at any rate in their initial enterprises before quarrels and rivalries had arisen between them, they also prepared a way of approach to the Gentile world. In Alexandria, where the Jews formed a large and powerful section of the people, some kind of synthesis with Gentile thought had already taken place. The Old Testament had been translated into Greek, and in Philo the attempt had been made to present the Jewish faith in a guise which would commend it to non-Semitic peoples. All this was of immense help to the Christian missionaries.

None the less, Christianity found Judaism too narrow; it was compelled to attempt a wider flight. The belief that God is one demands a world-wide acknowledgment, and those who hold it are bound ultimately to seek disciples of all nations. A God who is claimed to be universal cannot be confined to a single race, much less to a single territory. If God is all sovereign the world must be brought to serve Him. In embarking upon its universal crusade Christianity was helped by the fact that it had no central shrine like Judaism. Circumstances would have made it difficult for Jerusalem to remain the headquarters of the Church, even if it had not been destroyed by the Romans and a new city erected on its site.

The Holy Land itself seems to have meant but little to Christians before the age of Constantine, though Melito, Bishop of Sardis, in the latter half of the second century, speaks of a steady flow of pilgrims and of the relics which were produced for their delectation. The situation was not sufficiently stable for such efforts to be organised so long as Christianity was discountenanced by the government; but with the extension of the rule of Constantine to the East all was made easy and the Empress Helena, the mother of Constantine, herself set the fashion. Later St. Jerome established himself at Bethlehem and drew visitors from the West.

It was not for some time, however, that the Church fully realised its mission. In the first three gospels, commonly called the Synoptic, there is little about any extension beyond Palestine, or of any people but the Jews as possible adherents. The time was short, for the Lord Himself would return before even the cities of Israel had been evangelised (Matthew x. 23); so why think of any beyond its borders? On the other hand there is the definite statement that the Gospel is to be preached to all nations (Mark xiii. 10; xiv. 9; Matthew viii. 11; xxviii. 19f.; Luke xxiv. 47). When we come down to the fourth gospel, however, the complete, universal outlook has been realised (John i. 29; x. 16, etc.)—the world is constantly mentioned as the object of God's love and there is a sinister reiteration of the title 'the Jews' which shows that the Church had become quite conscious of its differences from them.

The birthday of the Church is generally taken to be the Pentecost which followed the Crucifixion, when the Spirit descended on the waiting disciples to equip them for their stupendous task. The experience of Pentecost for the Church, and for its individual members, was something so intense that in the strength of it they set out to convert their Jewish brethren to the belief in Jesus as the Messiah. The power of God, at other times, has fallen upon gatherings of men, but this was the supreme example and instance of its working. The disciples thrilled with the new life that was in them and all doubts and hesitations were swept away. At once St. Peter addressed the multitude and, in spite of scoffing and slander, many were added to the infant community. The members of the new sect still continued to conform outwardly, going to the Temple like other Jews, though they had in addition their own private worship. The sense of fellowship was intense, and each lived for all. But soon this happy state of affairs was broken into by the complaint of the Greek-speaking Jews that they were being neglected in the distribution of alms. To meet the difficulty, and to save the apostles from too much time spent in mere administration, the seven deacons were appointed. It was one of these, St. Stephen, who was the cause of the first serious trouble with the Jews.

Stephen was of liberal views, and had come to see that in the divine economy the Law and the Temple had only a temporary place, and, their service having been accomplished, they were no longer of primary importance. On venturing to express such sentiments in public the anger of the Jews was so stirred up that their advocate was stoned to death by the mob for blasphemy. Among those who were present and approving the punishment was a young Pharisee, Saul of Tarsus. Other Christians held the same advanced views and persecution arose which compelled them to flee. The apostles, as yet, had not apparently risen to such heights, and being unmolested they remained in Jerusalem.

Those who were scattered abroad by this persecution went everywhere, taking the message of their faith with them, and so the evil, in the eyes of the Jewish authorities, was multiplied. It was just as though they had tried to put out a fire by flinging the embers on every side—to start fresh outbreaks. Amongst those who showed special activity was another of the seven deacons, Philip by name, whose preaching in Samaria drew in converts from the people most hated by the Jews. A visit of inspection by Peter and John from Jerusalem brought the apostolic approval of his work, and so a stage of expansion was reached. Among others who were impressed by the work of Philip and his superiors was Simon Magus. His offer of money in return for the power of giving the Holy Spirit added a new word to ecclesiastical vocabulary, and the sin of simony is known only too well to all students of Church history. Whether he was also 'the father of all heresies' is less certain in spite of the traditional assertion to this effect.

A further stage is marked by the baptism of Cornelius and his household by St. Peter. Cornelius was already attached to the Jewish religion, but as a Gentile by race his admission to the Church is significant. Then came the final stage when, at Antioch, Gentiles were allowed to come in who had not undergone any preliminary training in Judaism. The growth of the Church at Antioch and the novel experiment which was there being carried on made it necessary that some responsible person, trusted by the Church at Jerusalem, should be on the spot to supervise things. So Barnabas was sent. It was a fortunate choice, for Barnabas had vision enough to see the possibilities which lay beyond the innovation; and also to recognise an opportunity for calling into service a likely convert of outstanding gifts. This was none other than that Saul of Tarsus who had 'consented' to the death of Stephen.

Saul, full of zeal, had been the leader of an expedition to Damascus to seek out and punish Jews in that city who had accepted the new Christian teaching. On the way there his whole life was changed in a moment by a vision of the Christ whom he was persecuting. Thereafter his abundant energies and zealous spirit were to be devoted to his new Master. But things were not exactly easy; the sincerity of his conversion was not at first accepted by the Christians—it would be such an easy way of discovering who were Christians if a pretended convert got in among them. But Barnabas smoothed the way, and now at last he found for him in this new work at Antioch a sphere in which his peculiar talents could be used. Saul had by this time been a Christian for about a dozen years; but so far as we know his work had been carried on rather independently in and around his native city. Now he was drawn into the full working life of the Church.

It was at Antioch that the 'Christians' first received their distinctive title, and it was from Antioch that the first systematic attempt to reach the Gentile world was launched. Its leaders were Barnabas and Saul. Into the details of the various journeys of St. Paul (as he now came to be called) we cannot, of course, enter. There can be but little doubt—unless our authorities have sadly deceived us—that his life and mission were the chief means of preventing Christianity from lapsing into a Jewish sect. There may have been, and indeed there were, other Christians of an outlook sufficiently liberal to wish the Gospel to be preached to the Gentiles; but none of them, so far as we have record, was of sufficient strength and conviction to hold out against the pressure of public opinion which saw in the Synagogue the necessary threshold to the Church. St. Peter expressed liberal views, and it was by his hand that Cornelius had been brought into the Church; but so far as we can gather (in this, as in most things connected with St. Peter, there is much that is vague) he was unable or unwilling to stand out against the more conservative Jewish Christians, and at Antioch had to be severely rebuked by St. Paul for his hypocrisy. Even the rebuke does not seem to have been entirely effective since in writing to the Galatians St. Paul does not claim that he had altered his conduct. Barnabas, too, was liberal-minded, few more so; but he also took the weak line of acquiescence.

It was, indeed, a grave question that had to be decided. Were the Gentiles who wished to be Christians to submit to the Law? St. Paul said "No!" Others went to the opposite extreme and said that they were to be received on no easier terms; a third party was for some kind of compromise. In the end, as we know, the party of freedom was completely victorious, and Jewish Christianity gradually faded away. St. Paul may not have been the first to preach to Gentiles, but he it was who, in the words of Harnack, "dethroned the people and religion of Israel and tore the gospel from its Jewish soil and rooted it in the soil of humanity".

A tradition, coming indeed from a tainted source, the so-called *Preaching of Peter*, says that the Lord had bidden the apostles stay in Jerusalem and its neighbourhood for a period of twelve years. At the end of this time, so it is said, they went out to the different quarters of the earth to spread the Gospel. Of such an organised effort, if it ever took place, history has no record, and the ultimate fate of few of the apostles is known. At Ephesus a certain John the Elder lingered on until almost the second century; he had seen the Lord, and was the author of the fourth gospel; but whether he was the apostle no one can say with any certainty. Another tradition, not of supreme value, however, says that John, the son of Zebedee, was killed at a much earlier period. About St. Peter's movements tradition has much to say; but, unfortunately, tradition is no safe guide, and the farther it moves away from the date of events the more detailed it is apt to become. The New Testament tells us nothing of his movements after the Council of Jerusalem, for the epistle which he wrote is indefinite. The mention of 'Babylon' (1 Peter v. 13) is held by many to prove that he was resident in Rome; but though this is possible it cannot, in the absence of early tradition, be taken as decisive. There is much that we should like to know about his activities, but the records are silent; we do not even know what became of the wife who shared his missionary labours (1 Corinthians ix. 5). Perhaps some heroic story lies behind the silence.

The end of the first age of Christianity came amidst persecution and threatenings, with much that was vague and undefined in doctrine and organisation. But the 'experience' was still new and the Pentecostal life effective. To these subjects we shall return in later chapters; for the moment we must discuss that great event which marked the period, the breach with the Synagogue.

This breach did not arise suddenly. It was the custom of the early Christians at Jerusalem to follow the Lord's example and attend the Temple worship. Even when persecution broke out over Stephen the apostles were evidently not considered as sharing his revolutionary views and were allowed to remain in Jerusalem. St. Paul always went to the synagogue first in his missionary tours, and though his experiences were often discouraging the last glimpse we have of him in the

Acts of the Apostles is at Rome trying to gain the sympathetic interest of the Jewish authorities there. It is important to notice that even at this comparatively late date there was no consistent Jewish opposition to the Christians, for the rulers profess that they have received no information from Jerusalem condemning Paul (Acts xxviii. 20f.), though they are aware that many rumours unfavourable to the 'sect' are in circulation. None the less, they would like to know what it stands for.

The inclusion of Gentiles who had not been Jewish proselytes within the Church must have made any real communion between Jews and Christians impossible; and no doubt this was the real cause of the split. Ill-feeling must also have been accentuated by the growing nationalism and hatred of Rome which followed the death of Herod Agrippa in A.D. 44, and the misgovernment of the Roman officials who succeeded him. Nationalism and religion were closely bound up, in fact they were but different aspects of the same sentiment. In times of comparative quiet it might be possible to tolerate Jewish Christians who conformed to the Law and attended the Temple; but the increasing seriousness of the situation naturally led to a purge of those who were not willing to give themselves up entirely to the cause of the nation. The first grave 'incident' was the murder of the aged St. James, the head of the Christian community in Jerusalem. He was revered by many of the Jews themselves, and his death was the act of extremists. It horrified not only the Christians, but also the Pharisees, who are said, indeed, to have regarded the horrors which followed as the divine punishment for his murder. Four years later came the rising in Jerusalem with the massacre of the Roman garrison and the repulse of a Roman punitive expedition. War to the death was now inevitable, and even the moderate Jews, much against their will, were compelled to espouse the national cause. But not so the Christians. They saw in these events the fulfilment of the Lord's warning and, deserting their nation, they fled across the Jordan to Pella.

This was the occasion of the final breach, for it presented the Jewish Christian with the choice of disobeying his Master or of abandoning his nation. His position was tragic; yet he had played his part, and was still to play it, in the new Israel, though it was daily to grow of less and less importance, until finally Jewish Christianity was merged in the general life of the Church or passed outside its borders into open heresy.

That the Jews should regard the Christian members of their race with suspicion was only natural. Liberal views such as those proclaimed by St. Stephen and St. Paul must have seemed to them a renewed attempt to bring in that Hellenism against which the Maccabees had fought, the tendency which even then worked strongly in the less scrupulous of those who lived among the Gentiles. Within the Church itself something of the same contest, at a different level, was also taking place. In leaving the cradle in which it had been reared the Church deserted the Semitic world and set forth to conquer that Hellenic civilisation which had already, in certain groups and thinkers, invaded Judaism. It was a kind of counter-attack which resulted in a mingling of forces and influences, and only the Old Testament, which the Church retained as its Scripture, saved it from being too much subject to the influence of the pagan world around.

Jerusalem, as is well known, fell at last to Titus, in 70, and its spoils were taken to Rome to adorn the triumph of the victors. The Jews themselves, however, were not without considerable influence still among the ruling classes. Josephus had, by a timely submission, obtained much credit with the conquerors, and Berenice, the sister of Agrippa, became the mistress of Titus, and so great was her influence over him that the Talmud actually claims that he adopted her religion.

Two generations later the struggle with Rome was renewed with even greater desperation, and massacres on an immense scale. Once again the Christian Jews, such remnant as had been left, stood aside—they " refused to blaspheme Christ ", as Justin put it. Jerusalem was again captured and despoiled, and perhaps in Christian eyes the delayed prophecies of the Lord's return might seem about to be fulfilled. But by this time eschatological dreams were already beginning to languish, and it needed more than the fall of Jerusalem to revive them among the predominantly Gentile body which the Church had now become. Rome took a fearful vengeance on her defeated rival; death and captivity was the lot of the survivors; the very name of the city was changed into Aelia Capitolina, and no Jew was allowed to approach it. This effectively cut off even the Christian Jew from his sacred city, and the new Gentile Church of Jerusalem was a very minor affair, and no one could any more regard it as the Mother Church of Christendom. The name of Jerusalem came back; history is not so easily wiped out, as Hadrian supposed, and the reign of Valerian (253–260), if the evidence of coins is to be trusted, saw the last of Aelia Capitolina. It may be of interest to add that the Jews once more re-entered Jerusalem in 614, when it was captured by the Persians, and tradition says that they marked their return by the massacre of some 100,000 Christians.

The generation which followed the Fall of Jerusalem is among the most obscure in the history of the Church, though perhaps if we could date some of our documents with greater exactness that obscurity might not be so great as it seems. The period has been likened to a tunnel connecting the Apostolic Age with that which succeeded it. Certainly the early years of the second century, when the Church again emerges into full daylight, or something akin to it, reveal it as very different from what it was in the years before. Development has taken place, and much that was indefinite in doctrine and organisation is already on the way to clarification. The apostles themselves have gone, and a new generation of rulers and guides is now responsible for the care of the growing Church.

The age was not a creative one, and something of the glamour and romance of the earliest days has passed away. The first generation of Christians had been so fully conscious of living in a new era, so aware of the power and wonder of the life which was theirs, that those who followed could hardly hope to sustain the same high level of idealism and attainment. But if the first joyous onset is over, the Church is now seen settling down to the age-long effort of proclaiming the Gospel to all mankind and of bringing all things into subjection to its Lord.

The glad knowledge, for such it seemed to be, that at any moment the Lord might return has also lost some of its rapture with continued delay. Some indeed make it still the forefront of their interest, and eschatological speculations are rife in many quarters, speculations which far outdistance the wonders of the book of Revelation, though not those contained in Jewish Apocalyptical works. Among those who were considered entirely orthodox the idea that Christ would return to this earth for a reign of a thousand years was firmly held. Forecasts of the exact date of the return were accepted as credulously by the simple as if an angel from heaven had announced them—such simplicity has persisted even into our own day—and in some cases faith was so strong that the daily duties of life were neglected and possessions were even disposed of. Such wild extravagances obviously called for some kind of check, and a later century reacted strongly against all eschatological speculation. It may be worth while to recall Eusebius's scorn over Papias's belief in the Millennium.

Among the leaders referred to above there are a few outstanding names. Ignatius is at Antioch; Polycarp is at Smyrna; at Rome there seems as yet to be no bishop in the later sense of the word; whilst of the great Church of Alexandria nothing is known until well into the century. But the Church has spread in all directions, and there were few or no provinces of the empire in which active communities did not exist. Of the life of some of them we have information in the writings named after the Apostolic Fathers.

If the heathen writers ignored Christianity, save for a few scornful references, a considerable literature from the pens of Christians themselves has come down to us, though again we have to remember that it is almost certainly nothing but a selection; much has, without doubt, been lost, and some, whose doctrinal or ecclesiastical outlook was distasteful to a later age, has been destroyed.

The literature which has thus survived from the early years of the second century and the generation before it represents well the age in which it had its origin, for it is still simple and earnest, childlike and unambitious. Even the riches of the Gospel seem not quite to have been realised in their fullness. The writings are in form a little desultory, and their doctrinal teaching is not entirely orthodox or exact, according to the requirements of later ages. There is no real attempt at systematic statement—in this they are like the majority of the canonical writings themselves—and the spirit of comprehension rather than of exclusion pervades their atmosphere. It is for this reason, no doubt, that later ages tended to neglect them; for it was not until the Renaissance and Reformation era that they began again to arouse interest.

One of the earliest and most curious of the writings is that entitled "The Teaching of the Lord by the Twelve Apostles to the Gentiles," generally known as the *Didaché*. This work was lost until a copy was discovered at Constantinople in 1875. It has two parts; the first is based probably on an earlier treatise concerning The Two Ways which underlies the *Epistle of Barnabas* and other writings; the second is of great interest, for it deals with the worship and organisation of the Church. From its obviously primitive nature—an itinerant prophetic ministry still exists alongside the permanent local ministry, and no distinction is made between bishop and presbyter—it must be of early date, probably somewhere about the turn of the century. It seems to belong to the neighbourhood of Antioch.

Of about the same date, or perhaps a little earlier, is the letter, written by the Church of Rome to that of Corinth, which goes by the name of 1 Clement, because tradition says that he was the scribe who wrote it. The main subject is the dispute in the latter church over the deposition of certain presbyters. Clement, who by tradition was a 'bishop' of Rome, though whether second, third, or fourth, is undecided, aroused much interest, not in Rome itself but in the East which produced quite a considerable series of writings concerning him. The fact that his epistle was by one who bore the same name as that of a companion of St. Paul (Phil. iv. 3) nearly led to its inclusion in the New Testament.

Another writing which bears an apostolic name is the so-called *Epistle of Barnabas*. This, too, was regarded by some of the Fathers, Origen among them, as Scripture; but it failed to find acceptance with the major part of the Church and so never got into the New Testament. That this was a just exclusion none will dispute, for the letter can hardly be by Barnabas, and its contents are not worthy of such distinction. The anonymous writer deals with the problem of the relation of the Law and the Gospel, and attempts to solve it, in part by an abundant use of allegory, in part by arguments through which the rites of the Old Testament are explained away either as never intended to be taken literally or even as included through the influence of the powers of evil! Such teaching could never have come from a companion of St. Paul.

A work of quite a different type is *The Shepherd* of Hermas. This is of an apocalyptic nature and consists of a number of visions made to the author, who was by some claimed to be the brother of Pius, Bishop of Rome in the middle of the second century. It lays great stress on the need for penitence for sins committed after baptism, and the seeds of the later penitential system of the Church may well have been sown by it. It is possible that the visions were not all published at the same time; but they seem to come from the first half of the second century.

Two other writers from this age deserve mention, both martyrs and both authors of epistles: Ignatius and Polycarp. Round the Epistles of Ignatius two great controversies have raged. Eusebius mentions seven letters only; but tradition knew of six more. The work of Archbishop Ussher in the seventeenth century showed that these latter were spurious and that certain interpolations had been made even in the original seven. Then in 1845 a still shorter recension was discovered in Syriac consisting of three letters only. These, it was claimed by some, were alone genuine. But Bishop Lightfoot's great work proved once again the authenticity of the seven, and the controversy is hardly likely to be revived, though some have even denied the genuineness of the whole series. The reason for this denial was the high place which is given in the epistles to the position of the bishop. This does not seem to fit in with the ideas of the office which were current in the Church when the epistles were supposed to have been written in the early years of the second century. But it seems probable that the exaltation of the office began in the East and thence spread to the West; this would explain the difference. It is notable that Ignatius, who was Bishop of Antioch, and regarded the possession of bishops and presbyters as necessary to the validity of the Church's life and worship, in writing to the Romans entirely ignores any bishop whom they may have possessed.

Polycarp was Bishop of Smyrna and suffered death for the faith about 156 when he was an old man of eighty-six. He was a disciple of ' John ', but whether of the Apostle or of the Elder is not quite certain. A single epistle written to the Philippians is all that has survived of his writings. It was sent with a collection of those of Ignatius which the Church at Philippi desired to possess. This single epistle may possibly be a combination of two shorter ones; but this is by no means certain. Irenaeus certainly claimed to know of more than one.

Thus the writings of the sub-Apostolic age were, like those of the Apostolic age itself, of quite an occasional character, called forth to meet the needs of the writers and their correspondents or readers. They reveal a set of simple, devoted Christian men who reached no high standard of intellectual attainment, and were lacking in originality, but having a very firm hold of the traditions handed down to them from the previous age. And that was just what the Church needed in their day. There had been a great outpouring of spiritual power and a speedy advance; the task of the men of the second generation was that of assimiliation and regulation, of consolidating the ground already won before fresh advances could safely be made; and they were ideally fitted to carry it out. Papias may have been as stupid as Eusebius affirms, but he was typical of the wisdom of his age when he declared that he did not think that he could get so much profit out of books as from listening to the living and abiding voices of those who had known the disciples of the Lord. So traditions were preserved and handed down, perhaps not quite so unadorned as we could wish; but doubtless with a real kernel of truth within them.

CHAPTER III

The Struggle with the Empire

THE subject which is to receive attention in the present chapter is one of considerable obscurity in regard to several minor points. Authorities, for example, are by no means agreed as to the charge upon which Christians, in the earliest days, were brought before the magistrates—was it as guilty of some specific crime, or was it merely because they professed the 'Name'? Again the extent and duration of the various outbreaks are difficult to assess and the numbers who suffered. Leaving such uncertainties on one side, however, the main lines are clear enough for our purpose. There was a definite struggle between two powers for the mastery. At first actual clashes were intermittent and casual; later they became, by a distinct series of stages, organised and deliberate, until the last great contest under Diocletian and his successors.

The combatants from an outside and superficial examination appear to be ridiculously unequal. On the one side was a great empire which included within its boundaries the bulk of the known world. On the other a number of scattered associations of low-class and uninfluential individuals. But what a superficial examination could not reveal was that the Empire contained already the seeds of decay; whilst the Church was full of vigorous and primitive life. In rising to meet the challenge of persecution the Church found its soul, and put its powers to the proof. So long as the struggle lasted there was a reasonable certainty that those who professed and called themselves Christians would be sincere in their profession. The merely nominal Church member, if he thought it worth his while to join the Church, would be scared away by the approach of danger. Thus the body was kept pure and vigorous; whilst those who suffered gave an example to the rest of endurance and faith, the flaming souls of the martyrs lighting the way for their less heroic brethren. Fellowship in suffering made a bond such as no other experience could have forged, and it linked not only individuals but churches as well. <u>If one member suffered the whole body suffered with it.</u>

The persecution of Christianity was a distinct break in the attitude of toleration which the Empire observed towards the numerous religions which were practised within its borders.[1] The Druids had indeed been suppressed, but that was because they combined politics and religion and were a danger to the State. But other cults, though they might be curbed a little, and if they became too flagrantly immoral definitely punished, were allowed almost complete freedom of action and belief. In the first days of the preaching of the Gospel Christianity enjoyed the benefit of this spirit of tolera-

---

[1] Tiberius, however, had made a drive against foreign religions, especially against Egyptian cults and the Jews. The latter had also aroused the suspicion and enmity of Claudius.

tion. It is true that the Lord was crucified under Pontius Pilate, but that had no significance as shaping a definite line of policy; it was merely that the weakness of a not very important official had allowed a judicial crime to take place, an event which could not be regarded as revealing the attitude of the Government. The career of St. Paul, so far as we have exact knowledge of it, is quite free from any incident which betrays animus against Christianity. Individual officials prove to be helpful and sympathetic, and the strong arm of the Roman power was sometimes exercised in giving him protection from fanatical outbreaks. Why then did the Empire adopt so unusual a policy towards the Christians?

In reply it must be remembered that at first Christians as such were unknown to the Government. Members of the sect who came to the notice of officials would be regarded as Jews, and it was not until there had taken place a clear differentiation between the Church and the Synagogue that persecution was at all likely to arise. For the Jews had a recognised religion. Later on, in spite of sporadic outbreaks, toleration was the usual attitude of the Roman magistrates and even of the emperors. Christians were always liable to be attacked, but why disturb peaceful citizens when there were so many other matters needing attention? Moreover the Christians came not only from the lower classes, but many of them from the small tradesmen who are among the most reliable tax-payers in any state. It is noticeable that the best emperors were among the worst

THE STRUGGLE WITH THE EMPIRE

persecutors, and they were persecutors for the simple reason that they took their duties seriously and saw clearly that the Church was a menace. But until the final struggle there was no consistent and settled policy which affected the whole Empire and continued in operation for any considerable time.

Once Christianity was distinguished from Judaism it was clearly an " unlawful " religion; since it was not a national faith it had no recognised status and all congregations of Christians were simply unlicensed associations. This in itself probably did not mean that they were illegal in the absence of any special order suppressing such societies (as in Bithynia in the days of Trajan); it merely meant that their existence was not acknowledged by the law, and that they were unable to claim its protection or to hold property.

The offence for which Christians were persecuted under Nero was that of arson, and by a later development hatred of the human race. Under Trajan it was membership of a society when such had been ordered to disband. After Trajan the question of conforming to the religion of the Empire became more and more prominent until at last it is the real point at issue. It was here indeed that the Church was dangerous to the State; it refused to accept, alongside its own objects of devotion, the worship of the emperor.

The decay of patriotism consequent upon the incorporation within the Empire of numberless races and countries, made religion, that is the official worship of the emperor, a very important bond by which the individual, especially in the army, was bound to the State. It was also meant to call forth his best services and loyal ardour.

Thus the Christians by their abstention alone were an element of discord and danger within the State. But they may also have been definitely suspected of the desire to overturn the Empire itself. The Jews accused Jesus of wishing to set up a rival kingdom. Did the memory of this or some revival of the charge, again perhaps by Jews, cause uneasiness in the Roman mind? Sir William Ramsay is of the opinion that the Church might in the early days have been "described as a political party advocating certain ideas which, in their growth would have resulted necessarily in social and political reform". He thinks further that "the Church proved unfaithful to its trust ... and failed to carry out the reform, or rather revolution, which would have naturally resulted from them". (*The Church in the Roman Empire*, p. 10.) It is true that the modern emphasis on the ethical teaching of Jesus as the main content of His message has led men to forget the apocalyptic element in early Christianity. Those who joined the Church did so because they looked for a new age and a new birth of society, as well as of the individual. It is almost certain that among the members of the Church there were wild spirits corresponding to the Jewish Zealots who were prepared to use force to bring in the Kingdom; but surely the majority who cherished the hope would look to a supernatural intervention, the Lord's return, to bring it to pass. To judge from the literature which remains the Church claimed to be a conservative force, so far as the Roman Government was concerned; though there are passages in Revelation, for example, which breathe out hostility to 'Babylon'. Clement, in spite of persecution, urges obedience; whilst the Apologists, as we shall notice later, were exceedingly anxious to prove that Christians were a law-abiding people, so long as they were not forbidden to practise their religion. None the less it can hardly be wondered if those who knew Christianity only by rumour, and malicious rumour at that, regarded it as socially subversive.

Once the Church had been brought to general notice by the attack of Nero its members must always have been liable to further molestation, and each successive outbreak would only add to the danger, for though lynch-law, and some of the outbreaks were of this nature, can establish no precedent with the legislature, it only too readily justifies the mob. But in addition to the mob, here and there local officials or councils, eager to demonstrate their zeal and loyalty, might inaugurate persecution. Most of them, as we have seen, preferred, once the real harmlessness of the average Christian had been established, to leave them alone. In some cases there was a regular system of bribery and blackmail, by which the Christian for his part secured comparative security, and the official a useful addition to his emoluments.

Most outbreaks before the middle of the second century, however, were due to causes for which the

Government and its officials were not responsible. Already in the New Testament Demetrius of Ephesus and his fellow craftsmen perceived the danger to their trade if the Church made idolatry unpopular (Acts xix. 23ff.), and the owners of the slave-girl at Philippi also saw the hope of their gain taken from them (Acts xvi. 19). In many cases attacks on the Church must have been aroused through such personal grievances—the sellers of fodder, as in Bithynia; the pagan priest who found his wares no longer attracting the crowd; the exorcist who had failed to drive out a demon; the relatives of those who had abandoned home and family for Christ—all these may have had a hand in such outbreaks; and then the Jews, though perhaps not so widely as some have supposed, were often willing to vent their hatred on the new sect. There were, in addition, more general causes; sudden plagues or famines, floods on the Tiber, or low water on the Nile, these were disquieting signs of divine wrath for which the Christians might be responsible, since they neglected the gods and perhaps made even the sacrifices of true believers of none effect. Besides, Christians were so secret and mysterious. There must be something wrong if they did not allow others to be present at their worship and meetings—it was not as though they were a recognised mystery-religion. So rumours grew up of cannibalism (no doubt a reference to the Eucharist) and of fearful orgies. In any case they were bad neighbours who kept away from the public festivals and pursued a course of voluntary, social isolation. Such people ought not to be allowed to exist.

The story of the persecutions can best be considered in two sections divided by the reign of Commodus. In the early part the Church's real challenge had hardly been understood, except by a few observers. In the third century, however, its importance came to be realised, and after some encouragement from the Syrian emperors it met with a severe test in the middle of the century, a prelude to the final trial at its close.

It was with Nero that Christianity flamed into the notice of the Roman world. Tacitus, looking back over a lifetime, describes in a few pregnant passages the events of his boyhood and the attempt by Nero to divert from himself the suspicion that he had been implicated in the great fire which destroyed half Rome in 66 by accusing the Christians of being the authors of the crime. The fire may well have been accidental; the suspicion against the Emperor was not; and so it had to be laid by some means or other. It is said by some that the Jews, perhaps to save their own skins, perhaps out of rancour towards the Church, suggested the scapegoats. Torture and outrage fell swiftly upon those who bore the name of Christ, and so far did Nero carry his policy of cruelty that the sympathies of the crowd began actually to be aroused for his victims. A regrettable tendency in the eyes of the Roman historian who considers that though they may not have been guilty of arson yet they were deserving of punishment as enemies of the human race.

Tradition says that both St. Peter and St. Paul perished about this time. If St. Peter was a victim, which is very doubtful, his memory has been substantially vindicated, for the great church dedicated to him stands on the site of the gardens where the more revolting of Nero's exploits were performed and where the apostle himself may actually have met his death. St. Paul, as a Roman citizen, was slain by the sword at a spot outside the walls near which also a noble church now stands.

Under Domitian (81–96) there seem to have been further persecutions. If the Revelation comes from this period there must have been a very sharp outbreak in Asia Minor centred round Smyrna; but the date of that book is by no means certain. At the end of his reign the Emperor, in a burst of wild suspicion, put a number of prominent Romans to death. These included a near relative, Flavius Clemens, who was charged with atheism and following Jewish customs, a combination which inevitably suggests that the offence which gave a legal colour to his execution was Christianity. His wife, Domitilla, was sent into exile. Another of Domitian's victims, Acilius Glabrio, may also have been a Christian; members of his family certainly died in the faith not long afterwards, as inscriptions in the Catacombs of Priscilla exist to testify.[1] It was earlier in the reign of Domitian that the grandsons of Jude the

[1] H. Last, in the *Journal of Roman Studies*, xxvii, p. 90, has expressed grave doubts as to the dating of these catacombs by de Rossi and those who have followed him, and refers to P. Styger *Die röm. Katakomben* (Berlin, 1933), pp. 63 ff., 100 ff.

Apostle were denounced as having royal pretensions. On being brought before the Roman governor their rustic bearing and horny hands aroused only contempt, and their avowed relationship to the Davidic house was not considered a dangerous offence. They were allowed to return to their tiny farm and pursue without molestation the furtherance of that heavenly kingdom on which their hearts were firmly set.

One effect of the persecutions under Nero and Domitian must have been to arouse new interest in apocalypse, especially among Christians of Jewish birth and upbringing. The Old Testament writers always associate deliverance and the triumph of the righteous with persecution endured for the truth.

Under Trajan (98–117) there is the extraordinarily interesting correspondence between the Emperor and Pliny the Younger who was acting as his representative in Bithynia. It shows the best side of Roman provincial government and of Roman sober tolerance. It also shows that Christianity was spreading too rapidly for its own good. So many, Pliny informs the Emperor, had accepted the religion that the temples were almost deserted and the sellers of fodder for the sacrificial victims were deprived of their livelihood. The steps which Pliny had already taken having made many return to their ancestral faith, he now wished for further instructions in dealing with the rest. Trajan, in reply, lays down the principle that Christians were not to be sought out and that anonymous accusations (things utterly unworthy of the times) were to be disregarded. If Christians are discovered they must, of course, be punished if they persist in their belief.

In this reign Ignatius, Bishop of Antioch, to whom reference has already been made, suffered at Rome; and in Palestine Symeon, Bishop of Jerusalem, was tried and crucified. He was the last of the kinsmen of the Lord to hold that office, and in his case the fact that he was, like the grandsons of St. Jude, a member of the royal Jewish house, seems to have been one reason for his condemnation. There was about him some element of political danger.

Hadrian, the next Emperor (117–138), was a person of great endowments, both mental and physical; but some defect of character prevented his ever quite making adequate use of his gifts, an inherent superficiality which just robbed him of true greatness. Hadrian was interested in everything, and even Christianity did not escape his notice. The two chief occasions, however, of his coming into contact with the religion are both dependent on evidence which has been challenged. When in Egypt he is said to have written a letter in which he states that " the votaries of Serapis are Christians, and those who name themselves the bishops of Christ are devoted to the worship of Serapis ". Such an opinion would be quite in keeping with Hadrian's known character, but its genuineness is uncertain. More certain, however, is the rescript sent to Minucius Fundanus, which some reject as a forgery. It lays down, in response to an inquiry from the predecessor of Fundanus as proconsul of Asia, that accusations against

Christians must be dealt with in due legal form, but that clamour and false and malicious charges are to be discouraged. Those proved guilty are to receive suitable punishment. The rescript seems mainly intended to stop annoyance to good pagans who were being harassed, and probably blackmailed, by threats of being denounced as Christians; but it was also a safeguard against sudden outbreaks and spiteful attacks upon genuine Christians.

Under Antoninus Pius (138–161) there were isolated executions, but nothing which can be considered a definite persecution. The most famous case was that of Polycarp, Bishop of Smyrna, who was put to death in 156. In addition Publius, Bishop of Athens, also suffered, and three Christians at Rome. One of these deserves special notice, for his case may well have had many parallels. He was a certain Ptolemaeus and he was denounced before the Prefect of the City by an enraged husband whose wife he had persuaded to become a Christian.

Marcus Aurelius (161–180) was by nature and by cultivation a man of humane and kindly outlook, and may be placed very high in that rare class of rulers whose concern has been entirely to benefit those placed under their jurisdiction. He aspired to make actual the 'philosopher-king' of Plato's ideal. In spite of this he was the most systematic and ruthless persecutor of the Christian Church who had yet arisen. Lightfoot declares that persecutions "extend throughout his reign. They were fierce and deliberate. They were aggravated, at least in some cases, by cruel tortures. They had the Emperor's direct personal sanction. They break out in all parts of the Empire: in Rome, in Asia Minor, in Gaul, in Africa; possibly also in Byzantium ". Well might J. S. Mill deplore his policy as " one of the most tragical facts in all history ". But there was much to be said for him. Among his early tutors had been that Fronto whose charges against the Christians are placed on the lips of the pagan assailant in Minucius Felix's apology. His evident conviction that the Christians were a set of godless and criminal men without any regard for the welfare of the Empire, even when not directly concerned to bring about its downfall, must have stained the mind of a youth in whom dutifulness was a marked characteristic. To persecute these traitors was a worthy task in a Roman emperor, unpleasant though it might be to one of his generous nature.

Among the victims of this reign may be mentioned Justin, and the martyrs at Lyons and Vienne, of whose fate we possess a very full description in the famous letter preserved by Eusebius. Among them were the aged Bishop Pothinus, Attalus, a " person of distinction ", and the slave-girl Blandina, whose courage and endurance amidst unheard-of tortures aroused the admiration of the heathen themselves. One disquieting feature of the outbreak at Lyons was the fact that the magistrates, disregarding the rescript of Trajan, themselves sought out Christians for punishment.

Under the weak and wayward Commodus (180–192)

persecution was allowed to die away. One case is recorded, that of the Roman senator, Apollonius. He is said to have been denounced by one of his own slaves; the informer had his legs broken, but the charge was investigated before the Senate itself. Apollonius refused to deny his Lord, and died by the sword. The lull in persecution may have been due in part to the influence of Marcia, the Emperor's mistress, who was a Christian. She managed to obtain the recall of certain Christians sent to the mines in Sardinia. In the end, however, discovering that her own life was in danger, not, of course, because of her religion, she managed to preserve it by contriving the assassination of her faithless lord and master.

The close of the second century marked a real stage in the gradual weakening of the Empire. It had obviously passed its full strength and maturity, and with the opening of the next century it begins, in the words of Gibbon, " to verge towards its decline ". The attacks of the barbarians from without, which Marcus might have prevented had he lived longer, were renewed with ever-increasing vigour, and, more disquieting still, they were matched by a distinct loss of ' nerve ' within.

The third century saw a very varied assortment of emperors, and in their attitude to the Church they manifested this variety. Some, especially those of Syrian origin in the first half, bestowed a mild favour upon it, a policy consonant with their eclectic outlook in matters of religion; some, these in the middle of the century, definitely tried to suppress it. But the majority were content to allow it to go its own way; other more pressing matters engaged all their interest and resources. These last belonged mainly to the closing half of the century.

Commodus was followed by Septimius Severus (193–211) after a period of struggle and civil war. Severus was supposed to be favourable to Christianity; but he did not show himself in this light after gaining power. His chief efforts, however, were to prevent fresh conversions rather than to persecute those who already professed the faith. The order which forbade Roman citizens to adopt Christianity also extended to Judaism, though there is nothing to show why it should have attracted special attention at this particular juncture. Although this order is often referred to as an edict, it was probably nothing more than a rescript, similar to that issued by Trajan, in response to inquiries for instructions from a provincial governor, and as such would not have universal application.

Caracalla (211–217), the son of Severus, although he was responsible for much bloodshed, does not seem to have paid any special attention to the Christians; whilst his successor, Elagabalus (218–222), was intent only on furthering the interests of the sun god of Emesa, from whom he took his name, and to whose favour he attributed his elevation. The next emperor, Alexander Severus (222–235), was but a youth of seventeen when he came to the throne. He had been educated by his mother, the famous Julia Mamaea, who numbered Origen among her intimates. From this source some Christian influence had gone to help in forming the character of the young monarch, and he apparently held Christ and His teaching in considerable honour. Alexander was, however, in no sense a Christian, and in his private chapel the prevailing eclecticism of the times was illustrated by the presence of figures representing, among others, Jesus Christ Himself, together with Abraham, Orpheus, and Apollonius of Tyana. In spite of this measure of recognition of its Founder the Church still remained an unauthorised association.

Alexander's career was cut short by a military rebellion, and his place was taken by Maximin the Goth (235–238). Maximin was a rude but efficient soldier who has received less than justice from Gibbon. During his reign there were sporadic outbursts of persecution and probably many Christians suffered, not so much for their religion, as for having been favoured by Alexander. Indeed, it might be said that Paganism and Christianity were alike persecuted by Maximin, for he laid violent hands on the treasures of the temples and crushed those who attempted to oppose such spoliation. Then followed the humane rule of Gordian (238–244) and that of Philip the Arabian (244–249). Philip was claimed by Eusebius as a Christian; but this is by no means certain, although he certainly showed favour to the Church. Towards the end of his reign, in 248, the Secular Games were celebrated to mark the passing of a thousand years since the foundation of Rome. This might have been an occasion for attacks on the Christians, but such do not seem to have occurred. The anniversary was followed by "twenty years of shame and misfortune", beginning with the murder of Philip himself in a military outbreak. Severe plagues came next which visited every part of the Empire—at its height it is said that there were five thousand deaths daily in Rome alone. Then came barbarian invasion and famine—two evils which were not entirely unconnected.

The burden of facing the perils of the times fell upon Decius (249–251). He met them by an endeavour to evoke the spirit of ancient Rome, and as part of his policy he revived the forgotten office of censor, hoping thus, in Gibbon's words, to restore "public virtue, ancient principles and manners, and the oppressed majesty of the law". The Church by this time had grown so considerably that it could not hope to escape the notice of a government bent on such a task of restoration. Its spirit was so obviously un-Roman. So persecution of a systematic character and on comprehensive lines was soon inaugurated. This, the first real attempt to stamp out Christianity, was alarmingly successful. The Church in its rapid progress had admitted into its ranks many who were not worthy of their profession, and as a consequence apostacies were numerous.

The method of attack was well planned. All persons were ordered to offer public sacrifice by a certain date, and it was left to the local authorities, backed up and kept to their job by travelling commissioners, to see that they did so. Those who proved obstinate were tortured, but the death-penalty was seldom inflicted. In some cases the magistrates winked at the failure to fulfil the conditions demanded, and gave certificates that sacrifice had been offered. Those who accepted them were regarded by their more courageous fellow-Christians as almost as bad as the actual apostates. But the certificates were a sop to easy consciences. Those who fled from their homes to escape the necessity of conforming suffered the loss of their property.

As has been said, the authorities did not often press matters to the uttermost; but there was an exception in the case of the bishops. These, as the real leaders of the Church, were more dangerous than the rank and file, and if they could be suppressed the others might sooner or later return to their allegiance. So there were many martyrs among the episcopate. They came from most of the provinces of the Empire, and the policy of singling them out was so far successful that much disorganisation became apparent in the Church. Some bishops were courageous enough to avoid arrest, even at the risk of being despised by those who had witnessed for the faith. Among them was Cyprian, the great Bishop of Carthage. He had wisdom to perceive that his life was of more value to the Church in Africa than a spectacular martyrdom.

Fortunately for the Church this fiery trial was of but short duration, for Decius was slain by the Goths in 251, and after his fall no one was anxious, for the time, to persist in his policy. The Church, although it was disorganised in many parts, and had lost some true and faithful leaders, emerged in greater strength; for the weaker brethren had been pruned away, and those who remained purified and strengthened by their experience.

The lull in persecution was only temporary, and after six years of peace Valerian (253–260) again took measures against the Church. He issued two edicts in 257 and the year following. By them all persons were commanded to conform to the ceremonies of the Roman people. Those of rank who refused were to be degraded and their property confiscated. The bishops and clergy were to suffer death, as were members of the upper classes who proved obstinate, though women of position were only to suffer banishment and the loss of their possessions. Public servants were to be sent to the mines. Assemblies of Christians were forbidden, and the catacombs were placed ' out of bounds '.

The policy of Valerian followed much the same lines as that of his predecessor—the leaders and persons of rank were attacked with especial severity, in the belief that their loss would cripple and perhaps entirely ruin the Church. There was, in addition, the new method of trying to prevent the Christians assembling together. The provision forbidding the use of the catacombs was defied by Xystus, Bishop of Rome, who removed thither, from their previous resting-places, bodies traditionally believed to be those of St. Peter and St. Paul. On this occasion Cyprian judged that the time had come for him to make his last profession of faith. Perhaps he felt that the Church was in a better position to resist than it had been a few years before when persecution had not yet purified it. And so he made no attempt to escape and was accordingly arrested and put to death.

The persecution raged hotly, but again tragedy overtook the persecutor, and relief came to the Church with disaster to the Empire. In 260 Valerian was defeated by the Persians and captured. Gallienus (260–268), his successor, immediately put an end to the attack on the Church, and also gave orders that the cemeteries, which had been confiscated during the previous reign, should be restored to the bishops. This is an act of very great importance, for by allowing the Church to hold property in the names of its chief officials he gave it a legal status and, at the same time, increased the prestige of the episcopate.

From the death of Valerian until the last great outbreak at the beginning of the following century, with which we shall deal in the final chapter, the Church enjoyed peace and security. One emperor only need be mentioned, Aurelian (270–275). He was a votary of the sun-god with no special sympathy for the Church, but on being appealed to in the matter of a disputed property in Antioch, where Paul of Samosata, having been deprived of his bishopric, refused to surrender the temporalities, he ordered the matter to be settled in favour of the bishop who was recognised by the churches of Italy and Rome. Here again the right of the Church to hold property is taken for granted; and in addition there is a manifest desire on the part of the Emperor to exalt Italy and Rome.

Before leaving the subject of the struggle between the Empire and the Church it will be convenient to glance at those writings which are called ' Apologetical ', for they were evoked very largely by the persecutions which the Church had to endure. The object of such writings was to explain the real beliefs and practices of the Christians in the face of serious calumnies and scandals, and to gain, if possible, the sympathetic understanding of their fellow citizens. They were addressed to various parties, to emperors, to the Senate, to philosophers, or to the people in general. But in each case, whatever the superscription, the intent was the same.

Such a proceeding was by no means novel. Philo and Josephus had endeavoured to explain Judaism to the heathen world; and in the New Testament the two treatises addressed to Theophilus by St. Luke had surely a similar object, as the emphasis which is laid on the favourable attitude of such Roman officials as are mentioned goes to prove. But in one respect, that of appealing to history in connexion with a religious controversy, the method of the apologists, although it is borrowed from the Old Testament, was something new in the Greco-Roman world. The Romans were, indeed, familiar with such appeals in the political sphere, but here were men who tried to claim that since Christianity was the successor of Judaism in the same religious system it was older than heathenism. In adopting this method the apologists, it may be worth while to notice, were the precursors of the ecclesiastical historians.

The attempt began with the presentation to Hadrian,[1] at Athens about the year 129, of the Apology of Aristides. The occasion was well chosen, for there are distinct signs of a less strained attitude on both sides. Hadrian was tolerant and eclectic in his outlook; whilst the Church was beginning to lose the somewhat narrow and aggressive spirit of the days of Ignatius. The possibility of compromise was being felt and the need for understanding. A rather different spirit, however, begins to manifest itself after Commodus, for the Christians then took the offensive, not, indeed, against the Government, but against Paganism. They no longer seek merely to explain their own point of view, but deliberately to attack the absurdities of their opponents' position. Thus a literary conflict was inaugurated which would not end until Paganism was finally crushed; and even then the conflict had to be continued within the Church itself, as remnants of heathenism raised their heads in the forms of various heresies. Paganism, it may be remarked, was itself stung into some kind of renewed life by the challenge, which it met in part by borrowings from its adversary.

To explain Christianity to emperors and statesmen was not a difficult task—that is, on paper; for it is

[1] So Eusebius, iv. iii. 3. It is probable, however, that it was presented to Antoninus, the next emperor.

probable that even if any notice was taken of such effusions by prominent people, emperors and so forth, they were but little influenced by them. To them as to the common people Christianity would explain and justify itself by the lives of Christian men and women. The attempt to make Christianity respectable in the eyes of philosophers, however, was a far more complicated task.

In dealing with statesmen it was enough to point out that the scandalous stories about the Church and its members were entirely untrue, that on the contrary Christians made a point of avoiding every manner of crime and wickedness and lived lives of great purity and self-denial. Some apologists even ventured to claim that they were the soul which held the Empire together, and that great blessings had already come upon it through their presence. In any case, they were useful as conquerors of demons, the common foe of all mankind. It was really owing to the influence of such agencies that the emperors had been persuaded to attack the Christians. Tertullian went so far as to claim that it was only bad emperors, like Nero and Domitian, who had done so. This was rather a fallacious argument; but the apologists were trained rhetoricians and tried to make the best case possible for their side; those who read their works would, in any case, knock off a fair percentage for the exaggeration which was considered necessary in all such productions. The greatest stumbling-block in the eyes of the authorities was obviously the Christian refusal to conform to the worship of the emperor and the abstention of many of them from the army and the usual activities which marked the citizen. This had to be admitted. But, on the other hand, it was claimed that they were the emperor's firm allies in promoting peace, and if their religion forbade them to offer him worship they prayed for his life and the security of the Empire.

The attack of the philosophers is disclosed to us in the reply of Origen to Celsus, and in the arguments of Fronto which Minucius Felix put on the lips of the heathen in his *Octavius*. They were scornful of the attempts of uneducated and ignorant men to solve problems which had baffled the learned in all ages. The philosopher alone could have knowledge of divine things, the vulgar were quite incapable of comprehending them. As such was the case the best thing was for the people to continue in the religion which had come down to them from their ancestors; it was at least respectable and supported by tradition. If God were to reveal Himself, as the Christians pretended that He had done, surely He would have chosen some better means than to appear in an obscure corner like Palestine and among a hateful people like the Jews. Moreover, the Founder of Christianity Himself was hardly a reputable figure and needed some explaining away. But even the Jews were better than the Christians, theirs was a national religion, and they had had a temple and sacrifices, even if for some queer reason their temple contained no idols. Christianity was a complete mistake, and those who adopted it made themselves miserable in this life in order to enjoy an entirely imaginary hereafter.

In reply the Christian writers stated the real facts of the life of Christ and tried to make plain their own reasons for holding the faith. They pointed to the Christian writings as giving a true account of the beliefs and hopes of Christians; these must be consulted and taken as authorities, and no attention paid to scandalous rumours or spiteful misrepresentations. Appeal was made as well to the fulfilment of the prophecies in the Old Testament, and to the working of miracles, to the way in which the Gospel met the needs of mankind, and to the lives which men and women were actually living in its strength. So they tried to bring enlightenment to critics whose scorn would hardly allow them to give a fair hearing to even the most convincing arguments.

CHAPTER IV

The Struggle With Heresy and Schism

IN addition to the threat which came to the Church from the Empire and the pagan world as organised politically, a threat, perhaps of even greater severity, came to it on the intellectual plane. This threat was more dangerous than the other, because the tendencies through which it worked found a way so easily into the Christian society; for they came in with the converts themselves. Outside attacks, such as persecution, purified the Church; the infiltration of pagan ideas could only enervate it.

Tendencies of this nature were at work from the earliest times; for warnings against them appear even in the New Testament itself. Whilst in the next generation they become frequent. Ignatius, for example, speaks of the seeds of diverse heresies being scattered abroad among those to whom he writes. There can be little doubt that many ideas of a mildly heretical nature were in circulation among Christians at the beginning of the second century, before their dangerous and deadly character had been fully realised. In a more extreme form this became more manifest; but the struggle with them was all the more severe because of the hold which they had taken upon simple-minded believers.

It needs a definite and strenuous mental effort for us who have been brought up in a civilisation which, whatever its imperfections, has been exposed to Christian influences for many centuries, to realise the intellectual background of the first generations of Christians. Especially have we to remember the exceedingly vague and hazy nature of their conceptions. It is true that a few fundamental beliefs were held firmly; but their implications had not been worked out, and no one had yet tried to reconcile such apparently contradictory doctrines as the unity of the Godhead and the divinity of Christ. Something of the mind of the early Christians can be seen in the immense mass of apocryphal literature which has come down to us, revealing a background which is not only crude but also pathetic, because these writings were fabricated to strengthen those engaged in the struggle against persecution, a struggle in which many dear to them had already perished. Some, no doubt, were produced as a substitute for pagan works of fiction; they were the religious novels of the times and, as such, probably never intended to be taken as exact historical records of the lives and adventures of the persons whom they portrayed. But in the course of time these romances came to have the value of authentic memoirs, and anyone who is at all familiar with the way in which they have penetrated medieval art will at once realise the extraordinary hold which such legends must have had on the minds of ordinary Christians. Their authors quite evidently had the adaptability of a modern journalist in providing their limited public with the kind of mental food that it craved. These stories were an attempt to meet the curiosity of simple believers as to the lives of the great men of the past; they were devised, that is, to supplement the historical tradition. In other fields also there was to be supplementing of tradition.

As the Gospel spread among the highly cultivated its simplicity called for restatement in some more philosophical form. Minds trained along the lines of Greek philosophy naturally tried to fit Christianity into their own special system, to see in it fresh material towards the solving of old and baffling problems. Faith might lead to knowledge. This could be done in a perfectly orthodox manner, as the Alexandrians were later to show; but at first the result was far from happy. Thus the various heresies which arose within the Church were the result of an attempt to supplement the Christian doctrinal tradition by tacking on to it various additional religious and philosophical speculations. These took different forms according to the antecedents of their authors. It was natural, for example, that Christians of Jewish extraction should carry over into their new religion such characteristic beliefs as monotheism and the eternal validity of the Law. Converted Gentiles, on the other hand, still retained all kinds of ideas which had formed the staple of their thinking in the days before Christ had become known to them. So long as the Church had no elaborate doctrinal system and had not yet come to realise the incompatibility of certain of these views with the central facts of the faith, they were bound to flourish. In addition to such heresies growing up within the Church—it was an accusation hurled against heretical teachers that their most fruitful field was among those who were already Christians—there were definite religious and philosophical systems, as we have already seen, which were serious rivals for the allegiance of the Empire.

Still another threat to the Church's unity was to arise, not in regard to speculative matters, but concerning discipline and organisation. Such questions, if their ultimate roots are to be traced out, were usually raised by the holders of extreme views; men of robust faith, but narrow outlook, who sought to impose upon the infant Church methods and standards which were beyond its attainment. With them zeal far outran discretion and knowledge.

Not a few of those who took the lead in heresy and schism were inspired by an exaggerated asceticism. No one would deny for a moment the need for Christian self-discipline, for training and subduing the flesh to the spirit; but such teachers went further and came to regard the body as something to be despised and even tormented, and the exercise of some of its natural functions as incompatible with the highest Christian life. Virginity, for example, was held to be a more perfect state than the married life. The apocryphal books are full of such notions; some commend vegetarianism, some press the avoidance of wine, even to the prohibition of its use in the Lord's Supper; many are notorious for denouncing marriage. These and similar views are really pre-Christian, and belong to those regions of thought in which matter, and everything connected with it, is regarded as a distinct evil.

The outcome of these various tendencies was naturally diverse. In some cases the heretical views were suppressed and those who held them driven out of the Church. In some cases where the matter in dispute was discipline or organisation, the parties themselves withdrew, although their views might be perfectly orthodox. A third species of views did not involve the holders, for the time at any rate, in the guilt and penalties of heresy or schism; both they and their opponents remained within the Church and there continued to discuss their differences until at length some synodical decision declared that one side or the other had no legitimate place in the ecclesiastical system.

The effects of the struggle against heresy and schism were equally diverse. But, in general, it may be said that, as in the case of persecution, the struggle tended to tighten up the Church's organisation and, in addition, to make clearer its doctrinal system and to define the limits of Christian belief. With both these matters we shall deal more fully in subsequent chapters. For the moment it will suffice to point out that the challenge of heretical views drove the Church to appeal to and study its own past, hence the growth of the canon and the increasing value given to the episcopate as the centre of unity and the guardian of tradition.

Ideas and methods which might prove unsettling were also brought into disfavour, and so eschatology, as in contemporary Judaism, fell into disrepute, and thoughts even of Christ's return passed into the background; there was also a growing distrust of the prophetic ministry.

The contest with heresy, however, did not leave the Church unaffected. In intellectual, as in more material conflicts, the victor does not escape without loss. Views may be defended with success, but in the process they are prone to be modified. This has its good side, for it will be admitted by all candid students that some portion of truth exists even in the most objectionable heresy—otherwise it could hardly make any appeal. This element of truth may, indeed, have been much more considerable than we should be disposed to judge from the records which have survived. But in the ancient world the defeated side, in either politics or religion, could expect but scanty justice; its views would be distorted and misrepresented, and even the character of its leaders might suffer a similar depreciation. So it was with heresies and heretical leaders. Once the heresy was denounced and crushed its literature, even apart from deliberate efforts to destroy it, would pass out of circulation, and so of existence as it ceased to be copied.

In order more fully to understand the nature of the Church's struggle and the extent of the danger to which it was exposed we must now pass to a slightly more detailed consideration of the various systems which threatened it. These branched off in opposite directions, thus bearing testimony to the central message of the Church, and by their very exaggerations or reactions witnessing to its original beliefs. There would, for example, have been no Antinomianism if the Gospel had not contained a message of God's free grace; there would have been no Doceticism if the divinity of Christ had not been openly proclaimed. Even the more eccentric of the heretical writings have their value as revealing the reactions in men's minds to the Church's teaching. Much of the speculation may be absurd and futile; but it is, with few exceptions, concerned with what may be called the fundamental problems of every age.

We shall best begin our survey by reviewing heresies of a Jewish complexion. These are mainly grouped together under the term Ebionism, a word derived from the Hebrew word meaning *poor*, or less probably from an unknown teacher named Ebion. Such heretics maintained the typical Jewish conceptions of monotheism and the sacredness of the Law in such a way as to contradict necessary Christian doctrines. Though by no means at one in their views they tended to reject the doctrine of the Incarnation and to look upon Jesus as a mere teacher come from God for the purifying of the Law. Some, indeed, accepted the supernatural birth, but not the eternal sonship. The Ebionites naturally refused to receive the epistles of St. Paul or the orthodox gospels. They had their own version of St. Matthew, which probably had very little resemblance to its namesake; fragments of it under the title of the Gospel according to the Hebrews still survive. They continued to observe the Jewish sabbath and other Jewish customs. Some of the more extreme tried to enforce the keeping of the Law on all Christians; others were content to be allowed to hold it for themselves. Midway between the Ebionites and the Gnostics may be placed the followers of Cerinthus, who held peculiar views as to the relation of God and the world and the human and the divine in Jesus Christ.

As the Jewish elements in the Church gradually diminished in numbers and influence, such views lost their importance. But it was not among Jewish Christians only that the problem of reconciling a belief in the unity of the Godhead with the divinity of Christ was found insuperable. A certain group of heresies which have received the general title of Monarchianism also came to grief over this question.

The title Monarchian is given to these systems because they insist that there is a single principle only in the Godhead, a position closely corresponding to that of modern Unitarianism. The first to proclaim such views was Theodotus, the leather-seller, a native of Byzantium, who came to Rome in the last decade of the second century. He accepted the miraculous conception of Jesus, but otherwise taught that He was a mere man upon whom the Heavenly Christ came down at baptism. He could not, however, be thought of as fully divine until after the Resurrection. In spite of being excommunicated Theodotus gained some following, and even tried to organise a church of his own. Among his disciples was a namesake, called the banker, and a certain Artemon. The latter carried his master's principles a stage farther and denied the miraculous birth. It was for views similar to these that Paul of Samosata was condemned and deprived of his bishopric by a synod held in his own city of Antioch in 269. Paul was a skilled disputant, and it was not without much difficulty that the error of his views could be exposed. His followers eventually merged with the Arians.

These teachers solved the problem by denying the divinity of Christ. Another group of Monarchians approached it along a different road, and whilst retaining a belief in His divinity denied any permanent distinction within the Godhead. A certain Praxeas came to Rome about the same time as Theodotus and, because he had suffered in one of the persecutions and took a strong line against Montanism, gained much influence. He taught that the Father was God absolute, whilst the Son was God as revealed. The opponents of Praxeas called him and his followers Patripassians, because they made the Father suffer. This implication they denied, explaining that the Father suffered *with* the Son, but not *in* the Son. But Noetus, who taught in Asia Minor, was willing to go even to the length of accepting the full Patripassian position.

The greatest name among the Monarchians was that of Sabellius, an Egyptian. He came to Rome early in the third century, teaching that God had revealed Himself under three different forms; as the Father in Creation, as the Son in Redemption, and as the Holy Spirit in Sanctification. Thus the distinctions which he recognised in the Godhead were merely nominal. A council held in Rome in 258 condemned his views, but they continued to flourish and to be regarded as a menace to the doctrine of the Church—as subsequent controversies showed very clearly.

We come now to a consideration of the type of heresy which was most dangerous to the Church, which, in the end, left the deepest mark upon it; and again we have to deal not with a single system but with a whole collection of systems united by the possession of certain common features. To this collection of systems the generic title of Gnostic has been given. At one time scholars expressed doubts as to whether Gnosticism was really a Christian heresy and not a rival and hostile philosophy. Such doubts, however, can hardly be sustained, as in these systems, or in most of them, the central figure is that of Jesus as Saviour.

The task which Gnosticism set itself was a highly commendable one, no less than to restate Christianity in terms of the culture prevailing in its day. The Gnostic teachers were by no means content to accept without question the ideas of God and the universe set forth in the Old Testament; these, it was felt, were characterised by Semitic limitations and too 'barbarian' for minds trained under the Greco-Roman civilisation. The Gnostics also rejected the whole eschatological scheme with the Last Judgment and a messianic kingdom here upon earth.

Students of the history of thought must frequently be impressed by the manner in which ideas may be held over a wide area and during a considerable period without crystallising into a definite system of religious or philosophical thought; sooner or later, however, they tend to be drawn within the orbit of some prior system. So it was with Gnosticism, behind which lay no specific doctrinal scheme, but rather a certain point of view and a number of common ideas. These ideas gained new significance by being applied to Christianity. Some of the Gnostic teachers actually betray Jewish influences, but in the overwhelming majority it is the Hellenistic note which is sounded most loudly. According to the traditions current in the Church itself in later times, Simon Magus was the originator and first teacher of Gnosticism. Samaria, from which he came, was certainly a centre of religious syncretism in the early years of the Christian era, and would provide an atmosphere adapted to such speculations. But it is only with difficulty that the Simon of Samaria mentioned by Justin can be identified with him.

It will be convenient at this juncture to say something of the special characteristics and principles which distinguished Gnosticism as a whole from Catholic doctrine. This can be done only in brief outline, as the subject is obscure and interesting mainly to theological and philosophical students. The most prominent characteristics arose from speculations as to the nature of evil. The Gnostics began their attempt to solve this age-long problem by asking whence it came, and found the answer in Dualism, that is, the belief that two opposing deities, one good, the other evil, are engaged in a perpetual struggle with each other. Evil itself, both physical and moral (they were apt to confuse the two), they found in matter. From this identification many consequences directly followed. For example, if the world is evil, being material, it cannot have been created by the good God; so arose the doctrine of emanations to provide a sufficient series of stages between God and the world. Again, if matter is evil Jesus could not have had a material body; and so arose the doctrine, found also among other types of heresy, that His body was only imaginary; in other words, Doceticism. As to man himself, he had within him a divine spark capable of attaining to salvation, but it was hidden in a material body against whose influence he must ever be striving.

In their hatred of the body some Gnostics of a Syrian type went so far as to condemn marriage and the procreation of children, by which material bodies were produced and the human race propagated, as the work of Satan. Some would eat no flesh. In general, it may be said that the acceptance of the theory that the body is evil worked in two utterly opposed directions; some, considering that its acts could make no difference to the soul, plunged into all kinds of immorality; others, in order to reduce it to subjection, buffeted and maltreated it by an extreme asceticism. The morality of the Gnostics was deterministic, for they failed to recognise any responsibility in the individual for his conduct, whilst actions themselves, since the distinction between those that were good and those that were evil was merely human, were regarded as indifferent. Such was the theory, and it led some to lives which deserved the condemnation of the Church; but it is admitted, even by its opponents, that in practice most Gnostics accepted the standards of the Gospel. The discovery in recent years of lost Gnostic writings discloses a strong ascetic element and shows that a very severe morality was inculcated by many.

In methods of worship, as in the attitude to the body, there was also a divergence of views. Some Gnostics attached very great importance to outward forms and had elaborate rites and ceremonies. Such an appeal to the senses seems inconsistent with the tenet that matter was evil, but no doubt the value of ritual in attracting and holding worshippers had been discovered in actual practice. Some of the rites were of a highly magical character and, in fact, to the ordinary mind, Gnostic and magic are almost interchangeable epithets. The better type of Gnostic, however, was more consistent, and rejected all outward forms as being unworthy of a 'spiritual' religion. In any case, knowledge and not worship was the road to salvation.

This leads directly to another feature which distinguished Gnosticism from the Church—an exaggerated conception of the function of knowledge in the sphere of religion. Those who maintain such an attitude are bound to despise the common people as incapable of rising to the necessary heights of understanding. To the followers of Valentinus, who were Predestinarians, these latter were damned from birth; whilst the elect or spiritual were similarly destined for salvation. A middle group existed of those who might attain to knowledge if their circumstances were favourable. Thus, whilst the Church welcomed all and sundry—a characteristic which provoked the scorn of the heathen Celsus—Gnosticism was exclusive. The intellectualism of the Gnostics is perhaps one cause of the innumerable writings which they produced. Most of these have been lost, but quite a considerable literature, mainly emanating from obscure sects, has recently been discovered among the Egyptian papyri. Apart, however, from such discoveries this exclusive tendency is to be found in many of the apocryphal works. These also illustrate the claim of the Gnostics to possess a secret tradition alongside that of the Church. This tradition, so they affirmed, had been handed down by Jesus Himself, after His Resurrection, to Mary Magdalene and the apostles. They actually specified certain links through which their special teaching was connected with that of the first days. The followers of Basilides, for example, traced themselves back to a certain Glaucias, otherwise unknown, who was said to have been a disciple of St. Peter; whilst the Valentinians relied on their derivation from Theodas, a disciple of St. Paul.

The number of Gnostic sects was almost legion—a fact which the orthodox did not fail to notice and to contrast with the single, universal system of the Church —and they existed both in the East and the West. It was, however, in the East that they had their origin and flourished most notably. There were important and early teachers in Syria such as Saturninus and Bardesanes; but it was in Alexandria that the most famous leaders arose, amongst whom Basilides, Carpocrates, and Valentinus deserve mention. These were all prominent by the middle of the second century, and strangely enough are the first Alexandrian Christians of whom we have any certain notice. The system of Valentinus is the best known because of the elaborate account of it given by Irenaeus in the course of his refutation. Valentinus, however, was by no means so unorthodox as other teachers, or indeed as many of those who claimed him as their master.

Gnosticism made its appeal especially to those who were perplexed by the anomalies of the world around them, to those who had looked in vain for the Lord's return (it repudiated, it will be remembered, the Jewish eschatological scheme), and in general to all who were curious, weak, and restless. Much of it seems very dull and tedious, with its elaborate system of emanations and so forth, but the votaries of 'prophecy' and the Great Pyramid in our own day suggest that such things attract certain types of mind. There was, however, another more spiritual side to the movement which can be seen in the beautiful hymn reprinted by Streeter from the *Acts of John* as an appendix to his *Primitive Church*.

Those who were influenced by Gnostic ideas, and even the initiates themselves, continued in outward conformity to the Church, and indeed hoped to bring it over to their views and to 'capture the machinery'. No doubt they held their own little group meetings and formed what the Communists would call 'cells' within the greater movement. It was only when the real outcome of their teaching was discovered and exposed that they were forced to come into the open and eventually to separate. The number of Gnostics is hard to assess at any particular epoch. Justin Martyr affirms that in his day, the middle years of the second century, there were many disciples in Samaria but few elsewhere. Gnosticism, however, flamed up into feverish activity in Syria, and thence began to affect Egypt where, as we have seen, its greatest leaders were to arise. The visit of Valentinus to Rome was apparently very effective, and Tertullian claims that the heresy was strongest at the very centre of Christendom. In due course, however, Gnosticism burnt itself out, and by the end of the fourth century it had ceased to be dangerous.

The real gravity of the threat to the Church from Gnosticism, especially in the early days, came from the secret nature of its propaganda, from the fact that it worked inside the body. By reason of the pagan elements which it contained it was calculated to appeal to those, both within and without the Church, who had been brought up in an atmosphere of Paganism. Although the Church repudiated Gnosticism and the various sects were kept at bay, there is little doubt that it was influenced profoundly by Gnostic ideas. This influence was exercised gradually and in many ways beneficially since its cruder forms were naturally excluded.

In the earlier stages of the struggle the Church had no apologist who was fully equal to the task of coping with the Gnostic teachers, the age of Christian scholars was not yet, and even Justin, devoted as he was, was not quite sufficient to meet the threat. With Irenaeus the tide begins to turn, though perhaps his lack of sympathy with those whom he attacked took away from his effectiveness. None the less he was an acute reasoner and had a very full knowledge of the points at issue and of the views which he criticised. It was not, however, until the Christian Platonists of Alexandria, as they have been called, took up the task that the colossal range of the problems involved was adequately recognised. But even the Alexandrians gave too high a place to knowledge and tended, like their opponents, to separate Christians into two grades, the learned and cultivated—for only such could attain to the true inner teaching—and those simple souls who had to be content with the bare elements.

In dealing with the subject of Gnosticism I have so far said nothing about Marcion who is often taken to be a leader in the movement. This omission has been deliberate for I do not think that, in any real sense,

Marcion was a Gnostic at all although he had been affected by similar ideas. He was apparently the son of the Bishop of Sinope on the shores of the Black Sea and came to Rome shortly before the middle of the second century. A person of means, he made a gift of some £2000 to the Church; his money was, however, returned to him when his dubious orthodoxy was discovered. Marcion was a skilful organiser, and he had a keen and vigorous following. The result was that a serious rival to the Church was soon in evidence.

Marcion was a realist (in the non-philosophical sense) in his thinking and did not trouble overmuch about metaphysics or even consistency. His attempt to combine the acceptance of the historical Jesus with a rejection of the Old Testament was impossible from the first, and no genuinely deep thinker would have entertained it. But he saw the difficulties of reconciling the revelation of the Old Testament with that proclaimed by Jesus Himself. In the end he declared that Jehovah was not the supreme God, the Father of Jesus, although He thought that He was until Jesus revealed the true God. Marcion laid no claim to be the holder of a secret tradition, one great difference from the Gnostics, although he regarded himself as a follower of St. Paul and held that the apostles had failed to understand the teaching of their Master. Of the canonical gospels he received only that according to St. Luke and then after certain expurgations had been made. He was, in fact, the first to have a canon of his own apart from the

Old Testament, and thereby he stimulated the Church to make an official canon.

Gwatkin once said that if Gnosticism was Christianity perverted by learning and speculation, Montanism, which is the next heresy to be considered, was Christianity perverted by the fear of learning and speculation. Montanism is usually counted as a heresy, but it is really an open question whether it ought not rather to be termed a schism, for the doctrines which the Montanists taught were sufficiently orthodox, as orthodoxy was counted in the latter half of the second century. Where they went wrong was in giving undue prominence to the Paraclete and in laying undue emphasis on the approaching end of the world.

The founder of the movement was a certain Montanus, who is said to have been a priest of Cybele, the great goddess-mother. About 170 he began his mission in Phrygia, always a hot-bed of wild superstition even in heathen times. Christianity was evidently widespread and long-established in the neighbourhood, for a sudden burst of persecution had revealed the shallowness of the profession of many of the disciples. It was so severe that to the more earnest it had suggested that the Second Advent was close at hand. The exposure which this time of testing had brought persuaded Montanus that the Church's system was too lax; his followers must be willing to accept a system much more strict and bracing. The right to make such demands he based on supposed revelations which were made to himself and his associates in the movement among whom were two prophetesses, Priscilla and Maximilla by name. He also laid great stress on the continued influence of the Paraclete, a circumstance possibly reflecting the influence of the gospel of St. John which had become popular in Asia Minor about a generation before.

Montanism caused much unrest and disquiet. But it made a wide appeal and even spread to the West where it is adorned by the great name of Tertullian. Tertullian was a valuable convert and became an exceedingly ardent advocate of his new faith. In Rome it gained the interest of Bishop Eleutherus, but this dangerous sympathy was checked through the influence of Praxeas the Monarchian. Of him Tertullian, with his accustomed bitterness, said that he accomplished two things in Rome on the devil's behalf, " he drove out prophecy and brought in heresy; he put to flight the Paraclete and crucified the Father ".

The extravagant teachings and prophetic outbursts of the Montanists did much to discredit the doctrine of the Second Advent and all similar dreams of a material realisation of the Kingdom of Heaven on earth. Such teaching, it will be remembered, was also repudiated by the Gnostics, who regarded salvation as the knowledge of God, not as partaking in a material kingdom. Another stern opponent of these views, though on orthodox lines, was Dionysius of Alexandria, whose opposition led him to deny the Johannine authorship of the book of Revelation.

I suggested above that Montanism might better be

classed among schisms than among heresies. We come now to consider two movements which caused no little damage to the Church which quite definitely come into that category—Novationism and Donatism.

The Novation schism arose on purely personal questions, coupled with the treatment of those who had apostasised during the Decian persecution. No doctrine was involved, and if any principle lay behind the treatment of the lapsed it is difficult to discover it; the question was merely an excuse for venting disappointed ambition. Two men of similar name were at the bottom of the whole affair—Novatus of North Africa, who was in favour of the lapsed, and Novatian of Rome, who was a rigorist. Novatus, after a quarrel with Cyprian of Carthage, went to Rome, where he joined forces with Novatian. Cornelius, the newly elected Bishop of Rome, would not listen to complaints against Cyprian, and in the end Novatian, who had been a disappointed rival, allowed himself to be elected as the first anti-Pope. He possessed a considerable following, and churches of his allegiance were founded in various places, some even in Asia Minor. One suspects that local disputes were tacked on to something bigger and that the defeated party in a city might endeavour to gain support by alliance with the schismatic movement at Rome. In spite of numerous condemnations the schism persisted well into the fourth century.

The other schism only just belongs to our period, but as it appeared before the accession of Constantine it requires treatment. Like Novationism it arose ostensibly over questions connected with a persecution. It was said that Mensurius, Bishop of Carthage, had showed weakness during the trial under Diocletian, and a number of groups came into existence of those who regarded him with disfavour. Nothing, however, was done during his lifetime. But on the accession of Caecilian as his successor schisms broke out since these groups refused to recognise him and elected as their bishop a certain Majorinus. An appeal was made to Constantine in 313, and he confirmed the election of Caecilian. As this decision was not accepted by the malcontents he summoned a Synod at Arles in the next year and again the election of Caecilian was upheld. Majorinus died in the following year, but the schism was not allowed to die with him. On the contrary his successor, Donatus, was chosen from whom the schism took its name. The Donatists, in spite of every effort to suppress them by argument and by persecution, continued to flourish, though only within restricted limits; they never covered the whole of North Africa and never crossed the straits to Gibraltar and Europe. Their struggle with the Catholics was intense and bitter and continued down to the days of St. Augustine, and indeed until the extinction of Christianity itself in North Africa.

The Church met the attacks of heresy by appealing to history. Against the secret tradition which the Gnostics claimed to have derived from the earliest times it pointed to the open and available tradition handed down in each separate church. The succession of bishops from the apostles themselves was a guarantee that the tradition was a genuine one. Thus organisation was affected, for the individual bishops came to have greater prominence and importance owing to this reference to them; they were the guardians of tradition, as was indeed the Church as a whole. Stress was laid on St. Paul's teaching that the Church must be one in faith, and it therefore followed in order as well, for they were mutually dependent. The continual intercourse between the different churches was of value in exposing and discrediting local attempts at innovation.

Those who defended the faith of the Church were not at all afraid to accept the challenge of heresy and deliberately to contradict the conclusions of their opponents. The Gnostics might say that matter was evil, therefore the world could not have been created by the good God; Churchmen replied that the world was created by God, therefore it must be good. So, too, they insisted on the unity of the Godhead and denied the degrees in the scale of divinity, which some heretics advocated. Again they insisted on the fact of sin and the need for redemption; salvation was something more than knowledge. In spite of heretical attempts to condemn the Old Testament they made confident appeal to it as Scripture, and alongside the Old Testament the value of certain other writings was coming to be recognised; to them also, as representing the mind of the apostles, reference could be made.

In these and other ways the Church met the challenge of heresy and schism, but its victory was achieved, not so much by argument and assertion as by the quality of its members. It was the common Christian who made possible the ultimate triumph, the steadfast loyalty of simple souls to the traditions which they had learned. On the other hand the heretical systems, and Gnosticism the most dangerous in particular, were overcome, as nations and systems alike are wont to be overcome, not because of external attacks but because of internal weaknesses. Heresy had not the vitality and divine life of the Church.

CHAPTER V

THE ORGANISATION OF THE CHURCH

THE question as to whether Jesus actually intended to found a Church or not has often been argued from the one side and the other. To the early Christians such a discussion would have been almost meaningless. They were so confident that the Spirit of Jesus was inspiring them that it was of no importance whether the actual foundation came before or after His Ascension; it was He who was responsible. So far as we can gather information from the records of the early days of Christianity its Founder followed no definite programme of activity and established no form of organisation. In order to draw men into allegiance to the great ideal which He cherished He seems to have relied at first on the simple proclamation of His message to the people who crowded to hear Him. This method was abandoned after a time as they failed to respond, and, in order to secure the continuation of His work, He then seems to have confined Himself to training the apostles, and to performing acts of healing upon such individuals as happened to come in His way. The nucleus of the future Church can be discovered by those who wish to do so in that little band of chosen disciples whom He gathered round Him and in whose training the last part of His short ministry was spent. The writers of the New Testament, and so presumably the early Christians as a whole, were not sufficiently interested in organisation to leave behind them any satisfactory description of its origins and growth. Christ would soon return, and therefore no elaborate organisation was called for. All that was necessary to meet their needs during the interim period was some form that would express the fellowship of the Body, provide the opportunities and apparatus for the simple worship which began to grow up as a supplement to that of the Temple, and see to it that the poor and sick were not neglected.

Pentecost saw the birth of the Church, but it was not in the minds of those who were then gathered together that its world-wide scope and all-inclusive mission was first conceived, but in that of St. Paul. He it was, in writings which come so very appropriately from Rome itself, who first saw the Church as equal in extent to the Empire and even stretching beyond its ample frontiers. That splendid dream had its birth in a prison. When, at last, his strenuous life came to an end, he left behind him a Church consisting of a number of small communities scattered up and down the Roman world. In many cases we have no information as to the exact manner in which they came into existence, though we shall not go far wrong in supposing that pilgrims returning from Jerusalem and believers scattered by persecution were among the anonymous founders. Who, for example, had been responsible for preaching the Gospel in Damascus and gathering together the band of disciples who were of sufficient importance to attract the attention of Saul? We do not know, and probably never shall know. Even the churches of Rome and Alexandria can tell us nothing of their real founders, except to repeat late and improbable traditions, of St. Peter and St. Paul in the one case, of St. Mark in the other.

The local churches came into existence in different ways, and no doubt they improvised different forms of organisation; especially would congregations of Jewish and Gentile Christians develop on very different lines in accordance with their different experience of organisations. The Acts of the Apostles and the epistles of St. Paul show clearly that there was no uniform system. In some churches the rulers and ministers are called bishops and deacons; in others such officials seem to have been entirely absent, as in the case of the important church of Antioch, where prophets and teachers are the leaders (Acts xiii. 1ff.). This rudimentary form of organisation persisted into quite late times, for at the beginning of the second century the *Didaché* seems to have been addressed to churches which had not progressed beyond it.

If we are ignorant of the internal affairs of each community so also we have no exact information as to the manner in which they were linked together. Here, too, there seems to have been a considerable measure of liberty and independence, though alongside it there must also have been some manner of oversight, a higher ministry on apostolic lines, which perhaps moved about from place to place exercising supervision and a benevolent control. No doubt churches which had had apostolic founders would still be subject to those founders so long as they remained alive. But if the various communities were to some degree independent, their unity was also strongly realised. The Church, like Israel of old, was the People of God, and each separate congregation ideally an assembly of the whole Body. The Great Church, to adopt a convenient term coined by an early opponent of Christianity, was made up, not of smaller churches, but of individual Christians.

In the earliest period, and in Palestine in particular, the Christians were apparently a Jewish sect differing from other Jews mainly by their belief that the Messiah had already appeared in Jesus of Nazareth. Those at Jerusalem still attended the Temple, and no doubt there and in other centres might join in meetings of the local synagogue, though it would not be long before they would start synagogues of their own.[1] The organisation as it developed was, in Harnack's phrase, based on " the well-knit frame of Judaism ". What made it a novelty in the ancient world was that it was an association of a social and religious nature lacking in any political or national background. This was to bring it into conflict at a later stage with the

---

[1] The word is actually used of Christian assemblies in James ii. 2, Hermas *Mand.* xi., Theophilus *Ad Autol.* i. 14, and of Jewish Christians of a later date by Epiphanius *Haer.* xxx. 18.

Roman authorities. In the Gentile world, no doubt, the associations brought about modifications in the Christian communities which resembled them in not a few points. But the Christian officials were not merely elected by the community in which they ministered, some kind of higher recognition and commission was necessary. In the letter of the Roman Church to that of Corinth known as 1 Clement the apostles are said to have appointed the bishops and deacons, though these officers apparently have power to fill up vacancies by co-option. The approval of the whole church is also required.

The gradual realisation that Christ's return might be delayed, a process which can be illustrated from the epistles of St. Paul himself, must have made some more elaborate organisation necessary to meet the needs of growing communities. There can be but little doubt that the collection and distribution of alms played a great part in the development of fresh organisation; of this we have an example in the appointment of the seven deacons. Many must, on entering the Church, have found themselves cut off from home and means of livelihood, and so, for a time at any rate, dependent on the charity of their fellow disciples.

As a second generation of Christians, the children of Christian parents, began to grow up, conditions would greatly alter; not only would evangelisation be necessary, but pastoral care as well. In order to meet these new conditions the ministry was of necessity altered in tone and function. A ministry of 'office', as distinguished from that of 'gifts', would become more prominent, and the bishop and deacon take the place of the prophet and teacher. Prophets may well have been a real problem in the absence of any fixed organisation and with but few formulated doctrines. How could any real test be applied to sift the true from the false? That 'false' prophets were a grave danger can, I think, be inferred from the frequent warnings against them preserved in the first gospel (e.g. Matthew vii. 15ff.; xxiv. 11f.) and in the *Didaché*. In some way or other they had to be checked. In the end the 'prophetic' ministry and its activities were strongly discredited by Montanism; itself no doubt a reaction against too great a reliance on a merely 'official' ministry, with its consequent tendency towards formalism. But much was lost when prophets came under strict control, for the impression must have grown that inspiration was a thing of the past, and that the Church was merely the guardian of a static tradition.

The Christian Church has no 'priesthood', save the one eternal High-priest in the heavens, and it was not until a much later time that anything resembling a clerical caste arose. The distinction between cleric and layman was less likely to grow up in the absence of a professional ministry; bishops and presbyters followed secular callings, though they might also receive part of the offerings of the faithful to supplement their earnings, which would obviously be reduced by the time which they had to devote to the church's business.

When the Novatianists, as late as the end of the third century, established a paid ministry it was considered to be a scandalous thing. But as the Church grew in numbers and possessions such a full-time ministry was bound to arise; and we find Cyprian, in this as in other matters a pioneer, ordering presbyters to give up secular employments.[1]

The organisation of the Church was hammered out in conflicts, both internal and external, by the efforts to meet the various challenges with which it was confronted. These, as we have seen, took different forms—there was the challenge to order and unity, of which examples may be found in the troubles at Corinth which called forth 1 Clement, in the Montanists, and in the Novatianists; there was the challenge of false teaching, of which Gnosticism was an instance; and, finally, there was the ever-present danger of persecution. The success, also, of the Church had its effect on organisation. The increasing size of the various communities, and the elaboration of worship, made specialisation of function a necessity, and in particular gave special importance to the bishops.

Specialisation of function went on at such a pace that by the middle of the third century we hear of sub-deacons, acolytes, and exorcists, as well as the bishops, presbyters, deacons, and readers, of earlier days. But it was not until the late fourth century that these offices were arranged into a kind of ladder of

[1] The rabbis, it may be noted, scorned to give instruction in return for payment.

promotion. Thus the clergy grew in numbers and influence, so much so that it gradually usurped the rights of the laity, especially in the matter of the election of the bishop. The bishop himself could no longer, as in early days, have a personal knowledge of all his flock; and in the larger cities his various functions were performed, under his supervision, by a whole band of clerics.

The exaltation of the bishop was rendered necessary by the circumstances of the times, and supplied a definite want in the Church's organisation. To face successfully the various evils some kind of autocratic rule was required, as well as to overcome the weakness which follows the absence of a recognised and well-established centre of authority. The steps by which the bishop came to be distinguished from his fellow presbyters are obscure; but a number of contributing causes can readily be suggested. In the first place, a college of presbyters must have needed a chairman, to use a modern term; though it is by no means to be taken for granted that the same individual would always act in this capacity, the presbyters might very well have taken it in turns. Hort has even suggested that the title 'bishop' represented at first not an office but a function, and that any presbyter might act as a bishop when occasion demanded. It was not a permanent position. The need for a president would be especially obvious when the eucharist was celebrated. Thus, by what Harnack has called "the most weighty and significant creation" within the organisation of the Church, the powers of the college were gradually transferred to its president whose office became permanent; and so the monarchical episcopate at last emerged. It would also seem that the powers of the higher, visiting ministry, to which reference was made above, gradually came to be concentrated in the presiding member of the presbytery. A link between the visiting apostle and the resident bishop may perhaps be found in Timothy and Titus, to whom the title of apostolic delegate has sometimes been given. They were commissioned, for a limited period only, to take charge of certain churches. Before the first quarter of the second century had passed Ignatius could lay it down that a threefold ministry of bishop, presbyter, and deacon was essential for every church (*Ad Trall*. iii. 1).

Once the bishop was distinguished from the rest of the presbyters his powers were bound to increase; for he constituted a visible centre of unity and was the guardian of the apostolic tradition. When the synodical system began to grow up the bishop was the natural representative of his Church in its deliberations. To the bishop the administration of the Church's funds was committed and when Gallienus restored the cemeteries to the Church, after the persecutions in the middle of the third century, it was the bishops who were empowered to receive them.[1] Then, again, it would be the bishop who would grant letters of identi-

[1] To judge by contemporary Roman custom they would actually be registered in their names and not in that of the society.

fication to travelling Christians, a kind of passport very necessary in days when hospitality was a great feature of the Church's life and there were false brethren who would gladly take advantage of it, or even enter to spy out the land. St. Paul had warned Christians not to bring their disputes into heathen courts, but to settle them amongst themselves. In this he was merely recommending a Jewish custom to his Gentile converts. Such private courts would be presided over by the bishop, with the other presbyters sitting as assessors. In course of time, however, the sole right became concentrated in the bishop alone. Then there was the question of the treatment of penitents and the readmission of those who had lapsed during times of persecution. After some divergence of procedure, and not a few abuses arising from the undue prominence which those who had witnessed took upon themselves, the right was restricted to the bishop or to those appointed by him.

Questions of discipline and the development of a penitential system, the rudiments of which are to be found as early as *The Shepherd* of Hermas, helped to separate the clergy from the laity as well as to exalt the bishop. In the teaching of the Lord forgiveness followed on repentance; but this was too simple, as Gwatkin used to point out, for men who lived under Caesar's government and measured God's mercy by Caesar's justice. And so an elaborate system which reached vast proportions during the Middle Ages was gradually evolved. Instead of confessing his sins in public to the congregation the offender ended by confessing them in private to the priest as the representative of the congregation and of God. The theory that satisfaction was to be made for offences committed gave fresh opportunities for human ingenuity to display its powers.

In the time of the apostles and the generations which followed them the ministry of women had a distinct place in the Church's organisation; later opinion tended to discourage and keep it well subordinated. This may have been in contrast with the prominent place which was given to women in some of the heretical systems. The Gnostics, for example, had a number of women teachers, and in *Pistis Sophia* the women disciples are so prominent that Burkitt suggested that the work itself had a female author. It was, however, in Montanism that they had the highest place. The Spirit paid no regard to sex, and women could be the vehicles of His messages just as readily as men. So the Montanist prophetesses baptised and celebrated the eucharist. The leading part which women played may have been due to their much greater social consequence in Asia and the adjoining provinces than elsewhere. At Smyrna, for example, the Jews actually granted the title of honorary ruler of the synagogue to a woman, and the "honourable women" from these districts, referred to in the Acts of the Apostles, will be remembered. In the romance of *Paul and Thecla*, as originally composed, Thecla preached and baptised, activities which were condemned by Tertullian, who refused to accept her case as forming any precedent for his own day.[1]

The organisation of the various churches was thus developing; and alongside it there was development in the Church as a whole. Consciousness of being the People of God on the part of Jewish Christians had from the first fostered the sense of unity and dependence—a sentiment which St. Paul had driven home to the Gentile churches of his foundation by repeated admonitions—but there was no formal means of expressing it. This came, like everything else in the Church's development, gradually. Neighbouring bishops would meet in synods for consultation and common action in face of some crisis or problem. Perhaps the memory of the Achaean League and the assemblies of the Ionian cities, suggested the idea to their latest descendants, for it was in Greece and Asia Minor that they seemed especially to flourish. There was, however, a nearer example in the Annual Assemblies in each province in connexion with the Emperor Worship. That they should be able to meet was a sign of the growing boldness and power of the Church. At first, as has been said, they assembled to discuss some specific question; later, and in this Cyprian in North Africa seems to have been again a pioneer, regular annual meetings were called together. But such assemblies could only affect limited areas and be on a small scale; the danger of attracting attention, and the

[1] He also declared that the author of the work had been deposed from the priesthood for composing it (*De Bapt.* xvii).

difficulties of travel, would have been too great for anything more ambitious. With the accession of Constantine these difficulties vanished and the summoning of the Council of Arles in 314 for the West was a step towards the really ecumenical Council at Nicaea eleven years later. With the advent of councils the element of compulsion begins to appear. In the age of synods each bishop was supreme in his own diocese and his attendance was, in a measure, voluntary, as was his right either to accept or reject the findings of the synod.

A further step in the way of organisation was the gradual emergence of the great patriarchates above the smaller sees. In theory all churches were regarded as equal, as were their representatives, the bishops. In practice the more important sees began to play a leading part, and some kind of pre-eminence was allowed to Rome as the imperial city. This was all the easier since the fall of Jerusalem had robbed the Church of its natural centre. Antioch in Syria, Alexandria in Egypt, Carthage in North Africa, also began to stand out. The case of Egypt, it is worth noting, was unique, for there the Bishop of Alexandria did not emerge from among a number of lesser sees; he himself actually appointed the other bishops as need arose.

The position of the Roman Church is so important, in view of the supreme part it played in the later history of the Church, that something more must be said about its rise to power. In the first place, it must be clearly understood that the Roman Church did not derive its importance from its bishop; the bishop derived his position from his see. In the letter to the Corinthian Church, written near the end of the first century, there is no mention of any bishop; it is the one church which writes to the other. Clement, whose name has become attached to it, was, according to later tradition, consecrated by St. Peter as his immediate successor as bishop, and then reported his appointment to St. James at Jerusalem; doing so as the latter was 'bishop of bishops' and ruler of 'the churches everywhere'. So, too, Ignatius, in spite of the enormous emphasis which he lays on the importance of the episcopal office, writes to the Romans and makes no mention of any bishop. In fact, it is not until after his day that there is reliable evidence for the existence at Rome of any official who can be called a bishop in the later sense of the word. The church there seems to have been ruled by a council of presbyters.

Rome was well-fitted to be the focus of the new religion, for it was in effect a microcosm of the Empire, as well as its centre. In Rome could be found representatives of every race and every tongue, not only of the Latin West, but also of the Greek-speaking East. Well might Juvenal, in the well-known tag, complain that the dregs of the Orontes flowed into the Tiber. The Roman Church until the latter half of the second century was itself Greek-speaking; and to it there came sooner or later everyone, both orthodox and heretic, who thought that he had any special message to proclaim. Moreover, the peculiar virtues of the Roman Church—

virtues which are already to be seen in the epistle of Clement—its comprehensiveness, its sense of order and proportion, helped to give it a position of primacy and made men value its judgment. It was also noted for its care for other churches; to Ignatius its pre-eminence lay in the domain of love.

The pre-eminent position of the Roman Church having been established, later traditions grew up to account for it on the grounds that it had been jointly founded by St. Peter and St. Paul. As pagan Rome had two founders Christian Rome must also have the same number. The tradition that St. Peter had anything to do with the founding of the Church is almost certainly baseless; and St. Paul, as we know, was not its founder, for a church already existed there before he could write to it. At a much later date, beyond our period, indeed, appeal was made to the commission given to St. Peter by the Lord, and it was held that he had handed on his authority to his supposed successors in the see of Rome. It was Pope Damasus, of rather evil reputation, who first made this appeal; before his day, although the Roman bishop had often been in controversy with other bishops, and had been severely handled by some of them, it had not yet dawned upon him that he had this tremendous weapon in reserve.

The insistence by the Church on increased uniformity, and the tightening up of organisation, although on the whole a necessary and healthy symptom, was not without its dangers. It tended towards an increase in the spirit of legalism, that attitude of mind which identifies human authority with the will of God and seeks salvation in the performance of works. It also led to a spirit of intolerance and to the doctrine of no salvation outside the Church. Within the Church there was a loss of freedom and spontaneity, and possibly the Montanist Movement attracted converts because it was regarded as an effort to preserve the liberty of the individual, and a testimony to the continued presence of the Spirit at work in the Church. Above all, it led at last to the creation of a clerical caste, with a consequent depression of the laity, and ultimately to an entire change in the conception of the meaning of the Church itself. This has been well put by Creighton who wrote: " There has been no *Church* since the end of the third century. There have been two bodies, one offering, the other accepting, Christian privileges." He also refers to " the Roman conception of the Church as an organisation created and ruled by the clergy, existing independently of its members, conferring or withholding salvation according as its rules are observed ". (*Life and Letters of Mandell Creighton*, ii, pp. 375 and 378.) After Constantine took the Church under his protection the situation became infinitely worse. For the alliance between Church and State to which it led, demanded that the Church, in order to be a ready and effective instrument in the hands of the Government, should be of a uniform character and organisation. Both belief and practice, dogma and government, had to be standardised.

THE ORGANISATION OF THE CHURCH

Before leaving the subject of the Church's organisation it will be well to say something about one of the objects for which it was called into being—that of worship. Worship undoubtedly played an exceedingly important part in giving to the Church as a whole, as well as to individual Christians, that courage and strength and those aspirations after holiness which were among the causes of its final triumph. Nothing more can here be attempted, however, than a brief outline, lacking in detail.

The recognition that corporate worship was essential to the life of the Church is found already in the New Testament, with a reproof for those who absent themselves from the assemblies. Such worship would be familiar to the Jew, but to the Gentile it must have been almost a complete novelty; his idea of religion having been the exact performance of certain elaborate ritual acts which would compel or persuade the deity to carry out the wishes of those who joined in their performance. But he would understand the social side of the Christian assemblies from his membership of similar associations of a religious character. These frequent meetings must have been of great service in keeping the Christians united, and in furnishing them with that encouragement and zeal which comes from the consciousness of a common purpose and of a common experience. The combination of worship and social intercourse, although the *Agapé* was separated from the Lord's Supper after a time (scandals were apparent in St. Paul's day at Corinth), seems to have gone on well into the second century. It probably ceased with the growth of the Church, and perhaps with the influx of converts of a higher social standing. Mr. Gardner-Smith has made the very pertinent comment: "If, for the last eighteen centuries, Christians had combined their devotions with their dinner-parties, how different history would have been!" (*The Church in the Roman Empire*, p. 44.)

The Early Church knew of two sacraments—Baptism and the Lord's Supper. These were no mere symbols, they were means of grace as well as acts of worship, with the emphasis on what God did rather than on what man did. Baptism itself, in the Apostolic age, seems to have been administered at once without any kind of preparation on the confession of belief in Jesus; this at least is the impression we get from the Acts of the Apostles with such instances as the Ethiopian eunuch (viii. 35-38) and the jailor at Philippi (xvi. 30-33). Later on the need for preparation became evident, and a definite class of Catechumans was recognised, to whom an elaborate course of instruction was given. Baptism itself was often administered by the bishop in person, and usually on a grand scale and at certain fixed times, such as Easter and Whitsuntide.

The Lord's Supper, following upon the *Agapé*, was the chief service of the first Christians. It was accompanied by prayers and the reading of Scripture. Those who were recognised as 'prophets' had the right to offer up prayers and thanksgivings in their own way, as being inspired by the Spirit; others, it may be supposed, followed already some kind of fixed form or outline, suggested, no doubt, by the experience of Jewish Christians before their conversion. The musical side of worship was not neglected if the custom of Christians in Bithynia of assembling before daybreak to sing a hymn to Christ as God was at all common.

The place of assembly was at first in private houses, and at Rome at least in the catacombs or burying-grounds. As Christians became more bold, and the government less suspicious or less active, halls attached to the house of the bishop became centres for worship. An apse would be occupied by the bishop and the presbyters with a table or altar for the eucharist. An important piece of church furniture was a special lectern or platform for the reading of the Scriptures, to which great importance was attached. Incidentally it was the reading of valued documents which led to their inclusion in the canon of the New Testament. The services must have been exceedingly simple, and if a modern Jewish scholar (Mr. Loewe in *Judaism and Christianity,* ii, p. 45) is reminded by a Roman High Mass of the glories of the Temple services, the early Church had certainly not the means nor probably the desire to stage such magnificent performances; the synagogue, and not the Temple, was the model to be followed.

The exact functions of the various orders of the ministry in the performance of divine worship are not by any means clear. As the system became established the bishop apparently celebrated a weekly eucharist in his church, and if there was more than one church in the city he sent out presbyters to celebrate in them. In this way the parochial system may have arisen. It should be noted that there was only one altar in each church. The later custom of multiplying altars did not arise until more than a century after our period. At the beginning of the fifth century St. Augustine is very scornful of the idea of two altars under a single roof. In early times it almost seems as if the presbyters, unless they were actually presiding as bishops at the celebration, remained in their seats as mere spectators. In his description of the service Justin does not even mention them, and in the *Apostolic Constitutions* they have but little place. At first a considerable part was taken in worship by readers, but they seem gradually to have been displaced by the deacons as the latter became more prominent. One task of the deacons, according to Justin, was to convey the eucharistic elements to those who were absent from the actual celebration.

CHAPTER VI

THE GROWTH OF DOGMA

IN the earliest days of the Church of which we have any record, such dogma as existed was of the simplest nature. In the New Testament itself there is little that may be called 'theology' if we except some of St. Paul's epistles, that to the Hebrews, and the fourth gospel—but even then St. Paul could claim that he had 'received a gospel' (1 Corinthians xv. 1), which had presumably some dogmatic content. The New Testament writers thought in figures and symbols; the task of theologians was to translate such poetic imagery into stern prose. But this task was conditioned already by the historical record which the New Testament preserves. Those, indeed, who composed it had this history behind them, a history " shot through and through with theological significance. No doubt it is their own spiritual and moral experience which enables them to appreciate the significance of the history, and to lay it bare; no doubt also considerable theological development results from their endeavour to extract its meaning; but neither their experience nor their theologising has created the history ". (Hoskyns and Davey, *The Riddle of the New Testament*, pp. 244f.)

Even earlier lay the achievement of Judaism, which

came to the Church as a kind of legacy from the past. From the Old Testament it derived that firm grasp of the doctrine of the unity of the Godhead which was to hold it to its course in the storms of controversy which were so soon to break out. Eschatology may have been a gift of more doubtful benefit, representing as it so often did, man's desire, when the present offered so bleak a prospect, to make himself secure of the future. But the acceptance of eschatology does at least involve the rejection of the idea that history is a mere aimless wandering, and affirms the belief that things are moving towards some definite goal. So, too, the Messianic teaching of the Old Testament carried with it in its highest aspects the conception of God as a living God; a God who does not stand aloof from His world, but will, when the occasion demands it, decisively intervene on the side of right.

The Jewish mind was not interested in metaphysics, and had the Church remained predominantly Jewish the need for elaborate doctrinal statements would probably never have been felt. But the Church, as we know, did not remain predominantly Jewish; on the contrary, the Jewish element was quite speedily overcome by the entry of Gentile converts. Their coming involved a different emphasis in the Church's system and compelled it to adopt a different standpoint. From this new standpoint new problems were revealed, and the old were seen in different perspective. "It was not merely Greek technical phrases, but Greek ways of thinking which were imported into Catholic Chris-

THE GROWTH OF DOGMA

tianity." (Rashdall, *Philosophy and Religion*, p. 176.) At first this influence had but a small effect upon the intellectual life of the Church, for the majority of the Gentiles were not drawn from the highly educated classes of pagan society. When these at length began to come in necessity was laid upon them to express their new faith in the terms of their old philosophic training. Some of such attempts were felt to go beyond what was reasonable and indeed to change the whole nature of Christianity. Upon the Church, however, the stupendous task was laid of translating ideas that were fundamentally Jewish and Semitic into terms which could be comprehended and accepted by Greeks. This ultimately involved the working out of a complete and balanced theological system. In this endeavour the Gnostics had already given the Church a lead.

Until this task was accomplished or even fairly undertaken much latitude of opinion was allowed within the borders of orthodoxy. Indeed the frontiers between what was admissible and what was not had as yet hardly been delimited, and even where such delimination had taken place the frontier was but feebly guarded. This wide diversity of views is not really surprising when the different mental backgrounds of the first converts are recalled. Such a diversity is even found in the New Testament itself; one need only think of the Synoptists and St. John, of St. Paul and St. James, of the Epistle to the Hebrews and the Book of the Revelation, to feel that all kinds of developments were possible by those who stood in the succession.

Because theology had not yet become precise in either its ideas or its terminology the surviving writings of the second century are full of statements which a later orthodoxy could not but condemn. The need for guarded statements had not been realised. Hermas is particularly dangerous, for he wrote as if Jesus had been raised to divine honours in recognition of His work. Furthermore, like many other early writers, he failed to make any satisfactory distinction between the Son and the Holy Spirit. The tolerant attitude of the early Church is seen in the desire of Justin Martyr to accept Socrates and others as Christians before Christ; whilst Minucius Felix, the first Latin apologist, is remarkable for the undogmatic character of his *Octavius* and the small place given in it to specifically Christian teaching. It need hardly be said that there was also considerable criticism of the books which afterwards became part of the canon; Dionysius of Alexandria, as we have seen, rejected the Johannine authorship of the Book of Revelation, and Julius Africanus the gospel genealogies of Jesus.

But the spread of dubious and novel teaching compelled the Church to take action; statements of a dogmatic character had to be tested and either approved or rejected. Such a course was inevitable, for life and thought have to be reconciled; and any system which claims to be based on a revelation from heaven must define its attitude to human learning. Furthermore, the practical needs of the missionaries of the Church required doctrinal statements to be multiplied. " Re-

THE GROWTH OF DOGMA

ligion can only be handed down, diffused, propagated by an organised society; and a religious society must have some means of handing on its religious ideas." (Rashdall, *Philosophy and Religion*, p. 174.)

Thus the growth of dogma was not the consequence of an undue interest in abstract propositions, such a stage was to come later, but of practical needs; on the one hand of excluding dangerous heresies and ignorant misstatements, on the other of providing for the handing down of the traditional faith to the generations which were yet to come.

The first great period of conflict with heresy was the century which stretched from about 150 to 250; and during that century Christian thought became increasingly self-conscious and definite. In a sense the area of the conflict was restricted; the ground upon which it was fought was the doctrine of the Godhead, and the relation of the Son to the Father. The later, Christological, controversies which dealt with the relation of the divine and the human in Christ lay in the future, as did indeed the Arian controversy which filled up most of the fourth century.

The doctrine of the unity of the Godhead had to be preserved against Gnostic speculations which involved all manner of emanations and subsidiary beings of a semi-divine nature. So, too, the refusal of the Monarchians to recognise any but temporary divisions within the unity had to be met. Primitive man always tends to polytheism; to a belief, that is, in a supreme God so exalted that the affairs of man and his world cannot enter into His survey, and alongside Him a number of lesser deities whose range of interests is more confined; it may, indeed, be restricted to those of the clan or nation. To think of God as a mere abstraction is also the temptation of the philosopher who tends on the one hand so to emphasise His immanence as to lead to Pantheism, or, on the other, his transcendence as to lead to Deism. The object of Christian theology was to preserve both aspects of the divine nature and, at the same time, to represent God as one who cared for His creatures so much that He had revealed Himself in a form which they could understand by coming down in the person of His Son and sharing their life. The needs of mankind for redemption and salvation could not have been satisfied by the visit to the earth of one who bore merely an imaginary body, as the Docetics taught; of a mere emanation from the Godhead, as the Gnostics taught; or even of the Father Himself wearing a 'mask', as Sabellius taught. So the great question had to be faced: If Christ is to be worshipped is He worshipped as God, without qualification? And, if so, how can the unity of the Godhead be maintained?

The Jews might shelve many inconvenient and, to them, unimportant metaphysical questions, but once Christianity came into the main stream of the Greek world such evasion could no longer be tolerated; the philosophical Hellenic mind would demand to know the exact implications of the doctrine of the Incarnation which lay at the root of the Church's life. In

THE GROWTH OF DOGMA

putting forward this demand Hellenism did Christianity a profound service. Furthermore, not only did it insist on raising these metaphysical issues, but it also provided the language in which Christianity could most effectively be stated for those demanding something more than merely practical instruction, those to whom conduct and theory must ever be allied. All attempts to express religious experience in the terms of human language must, of course, be inadequate, but the Greeks most nearly approached the production of a perfect medium.

In demanding some kind of explanation of Christ's person the Greeks were nearer to the original balance of the Gospel message than many modern thinkers, especially in Germany, would generally be disposed to allow. Among the early Christians there was surprisingly little emphasis on the actual teaching of Jesus; to be a Christian meant acceptance of Jesus, not so much as an instructor, but as Lord; He is from the first the object of the religion, not its prophet; and what He was, rather than what He said or even accomplished, stood foremost in the consciousness of the believer. The historical figure was accepted and emphasised; but the vital, compelling fact was the realised presence of Jesus dwelling in His Church.

The first attempt to account for the Incarnation on philosophical grounds came through what is called the Logos Theology. Logos is, of course, the term used in John i. 1ff. to describe the Son. By the English versions it is translated as 'Word'; but it can also mean 'reason' as well as utterance. Those who followed out the line of thought which this double meaning suggested adopted the Stoic idea of the Divine Reason ever existing in the Father, but uttered at length when the Son came down among men. Thus a link was provided between God and the world; but at the price, so it might seem, of making the Son a species of secondary God, a danger of which Justin was aware and against which he tried to guard himself. This species of explanation was naturally popular with the Apologists who wrote to defend Christianity and commend it to educated pagans. In their anxiety to make it attractive they over-emphasised, at times, the importance of the Logos as revealing God, and rather left on one side His work of redemption. They regarded the problem too much from the cosmological point of view, and too little in the light of man's needs; a natural error in those who adopted a philosophical line of approach. A more adequate method was inaugurated by Irenaeus.

Irenaeus is one of the outstanding figures in the history of Christian doctrine. Streeter, to whom he was 'the father of systematic theology', regarded him as representing " not apostolic Christianity, but rather a critical stage in a process of standardisation of beliefs and institutions " (in *Cambridge Ancient History*, xi, p. 254). His strength lay in a complete knowledge of what had been written by those who had gone before him, as well as in a caution and balance which many of them had not possessed. He made considerable use

THE GROWTH OF DOGMA

of the writings which in his day were coming to be recognised as canonical alongside the Old Testament. By emphasising the divine Sonship he prevented speculation from developing in a dangerous direction, and raised the Logos theology to a new level. None the less, in spite of the work of Irenaeus, there were many difficulties still to be removed. If the Logos is identical with the Father, He is hardly a person, but rather an attribute; if the Logos is derived from God He must be inferior to Him and, to use a theological term, subordinate to Him. These difficulties were faced by a great series of teachers connected with the Church of Alexandria.

Under the Empire Alexandria gradually displaced Athens as the centre of living culture; it was more central and more settled, and the great library with its band of teachers and students was well fitted to foster the intellectual life of a wide area. The strong Jewish element there had already made itself felt as a force within its own sphere. It was in Alexandria that the Old Testament had been translated into Greek, and there, too, that Philo had attempted the task of commending Hebrew religion and culture to the world of Greece and Rome. In some kind of spiritual succession to the earlier Jewish teachers there had now arisen in Alexandria a Christian Catechetical School. It first became famous under Clement at the end of the second century; though the work of Pantaenus, his master, whose writings have all perished, ought not to be forgotten. Clement possessed wide and comprehensive learning, but he cannot rank as a really deep or systematic thinker. His habit was to deal with special points which interested him, rather than to face truth as a whole. To him, however, Christ was the Truth, and Christianity the final philosophy. Other philosophies had indeed caught glimpses of the truth, but only because Christ, to that extent, had shined upon them. It may well be imagined that such an approach to the Gospel, although it might make an immense appeal to the learned and intellectual, could have but little meaning for the mass of mankind. The Christian Gnostic, as we saw above, shared a little in the fault of his less orthodox brother in giving to knowledge too high a place in the scheme of things.

Clement's successor as head of the school was his pupil, Origen, one of the greatest and most daring thinkers of all time. His learning was even more vast than that of Clement, whom he far excelled in profundity of thought. Not only was his thought more profound, however, but he had also a much more complete appreciation of the need for a systematic and comprehensive treatment of truth. If Christianity is the final philosophy it must be shown to cover the whole of life and thought. Origen became head of the school when only eighteen years old, and he lived to a considerable age. His career was one of variegated fortunes, for he had much to endure not only from the opposition of the heathen, but also from the suspicion of his fellow Christians. The latter part of his life was spent in Caesarea.

In doctrine Origen set himself the task of combating two dangerous theories; on the one hand that the persons of the Father and the Son are 'confused', and on the other that they have separate natures. This he accomplished by the theory known as the eternal generation of the Son. Other speculations of his brought much controversy. He believed, with Plato, that all souls are pre-existent, and that the human soul of Christ was like other souls in this respect. Such a suggestion opened the door to much unprofitable wrangling, and those who claimed to be his followers by pressing his teaching beyond the limits which he would probably have laid down, caused him to be regarded as a dangerous, if not heretical, teacher.

The activities of Origen in Christian learning were by no means confined to doctrine and related subjects; he did pioneer work in textual criticism and in the exegesis of the Bible. Unfortunately, his methods of interpretation, in accordance with the school in which he had been trained, were somewhat fanciful. The revelation contained in Scripture was, it need hardly be said, accepted in all its fullness, but the use of allegory led to all kinds of futility.

The thought of our Lord as the Logos tended, during the first Christian centuries, to make men ignore the work of the Holy Spirit. There was a belief in His person, but it was seldom put into words, and little thought had as yet been devoted to His relation to the other persons of the Trinity, or even to the individual believer. The absence of interest is remarkable in such a profound thinker as Origen; but it prevented controversy such as developed in the post-Nicene age.

Contemporary with Clement and Origen in Alexandria two great teachers had arisen in the western part of North Africa, where Latin Christianity, as an intellectual force, may be said to have been evolved. Tertullian, the first and greater of the two, was born in Carthage, but practised as a lawyer in Rome. To the end he had the legal mind, though this did not prevent his writings becoming obscure when feeling stirred the depths of his fanatical nature. He was a foe to any kind of half-measure, and what he held he held with intense fervour; the saying of Caesar about Brutus *quidquid vult, valde vult* has been applied to him, and it certainly fits. His greatest achievement was to coin a new theological terminology for the Latin West, and if in doing so he tended to too much rigidity that could not have been avoided by another; rigidity waited unavoidably upon the attempt to translate religious and metaphysical terms from Greek into Latin. Tertullian's stern and uncompromising nature led him at the last to embrace the Montanist version of Christian life and teaching and to engage in bitter controversy with all those who were unwilling to follow him.

Cyprian was a much more attractive and practical sort of person. Like Tertullian, whose writings he read daily and whom he called his master, he had been a lawyer; he did not indeed become a Christian until he was well

THE GROWTH OF DOGMA

past forty. His writings were concerned mainly with problems of administration, and lay down principles concerning Church order and discipline, which had no little effect on the development of Western Christendom. Although he held his views as tenaciously as Tertullian, he had a more comprehensive spirit and was willing to listen to the other side in any controversy, even if his own views remained the same at the end. Firmness without harshness may be said to represent his characteristic point of view.

Whilst scholars and thinkers were thus seeking to trace out the implications of the Christian faith in its philosophical bearings and endeavouring to give a Greek or Latin form to its fundamentally Semitic content, the need of the common people for some simple expression of their faith, both as a test for entry into the Church and as a basis for further instruction, had not been forgotten. It was met by the formulation of creeds.

In the New Testament there are various credal forms of a very simple nature. The acceptance of Jesus as Lord (Rom. x. 9; 1 Cor. xii. 3) seems to be the basis of them all; but fuller details are found in passages such as 1 Cor. xv. 3f.; Phil. ii. 5ff.; 2 Tim. ii. 8, and 1 Peter iii. 13ff. There is also an adumbration of the threefold form of later creeds, the confession of the Trinity, in Matt xxviii. 19, and 2 Cor. xiii. 13. There are some scholars, indeed, who think that two distinct types of creed developed in early days, one expressing belief in Christ, the other of faith in the Trinity, and that the fullness of detail under the second article of later formularies is due to the combination of the two.

Beyond the elementary need for confessing belief in Jesus as Lord and in the threefold nature of the Godhead the various creeds developed in different ways. The freedom and variety of expression, so characteristic of the first ages of the Church, is well seen in this matter also. Perhaps the earliest form which has survived is an Egyptian Creed which runs as follows:

> I believe in God, the Father, the Almighty,
> And in Christ Jesus, His only begotten Son, our Lord,
> And in the Holy Spirit, the holy Church, the resurrection of the flesh.

It is possible, however, that this is a simplification of the famous creed of the West, the Roman Creed which, with a few additions and alterations, we still use under the name of the Apostles' Creed. The West found a formula to suit it much earlier than the East and preserved it with but little change. In the East there were many and various credal documents, which went into much fuller detail; but they belong to a later period than the Ante-Nicene age with which we are now concerned, although their origins, without doubt, lie in our period could we but discover them.

The creeds were first used in all probability as forms to be accepted at baptism by those who wished to make an open confession of their faith. But other occasions for open confession would no doubt be used in early

THE GROWTH OF DOGMA

days, in the eucharist for example. In fact it may be surmised that the development of credal forms was largely influenced and guided by liturgical needs, the summing up of the Church's faith for utterance in the presence of God and the assembled Church in language of a ceremonial nature. The regular recital of the true faith would be a safeguard against the spread of errors and misapprehensions, as well as a stimulus to a life worthy of so high a profession.

The importance of the Scriptures as the source and basis of doctrine is so great that this chapter may fittingly conclude with a brief sketch of the growth of what is known as the canon of the New Testament, that is, the list of writings accepted as authoritative.

The Early Church knew of but one canon, that of the Old Testament, and no thought of any other collection of Scriptures probably entered the minds of anyone in that period—the Lord would return at any moment, so what need of further books. Those who wrote what are now accepted as canonical writings could have had no idea that their effusions, the product for the most part of the special needs of the hour, would ever be preserved, much less placed beside the books of the Old Testament. To this statement there is, however, one striking exception, and that is the writer of the only book in the New Testament which has the nature of a prophecy—the book of Revelation. Its author definitely claims to be inspired, and even goes so far as to append a curse to his book against anyone who should dare to take away from or add to its words (xxii. 18).

The manner in which the second canon grew up must have been perfectly simple. Those churches which possessed letters from the apostles or other leaders would naturally preserve them with great care, and from time to time they would be read aloud at the meetings of the congregation alongside the older Scriptures. There would also be, as time went on, an exchange of such letters between the different churches. (We have an illustration, if not an actual example, in the request of the Philippians for copies of the letters of Ignatius to be sent to them at the beginning of the second century.) In addition to collections of letters of apostolic men there would be the need, from quite early days, of some account of the life of the Lord for the instruction of converts. At first this may well have been oral, but in process of time it would be written down. No doubt a different form would be used, with fundamental agreement, in each church. It is interesting and instructive to note that Clement of Rome, at the end of the first century, and Polycarp of Smyrna, a few years later, both quote sayings of the Lord in a form which is not to be found in any of the present gospels. These gospels themselves probably survived when others perished, because they were current in the more important churches. Mark appears to have been adopted in Rome, while Matthew (which incorporates much of Mark) has connexions with Antioch. The fourth gospel,

THE GROWTH OF DOGMA

whatever its authorship, depended on Ephesus. The two works attributed to St. Luke, the gospel and the Acts of the Apostles, are not quite so easy to locate, but their importance must have been recognised from the first.

The Church was first aroused to the need for some kind of an authorised collection of books by the challenge of heresy. If doctrinal questions were to be settled by an appeal to records the records themselves must be specified. Strangely enough no official decision of the whole Church was ever issued. The question was decided by the general consensus of the individual churches and the judgment of scholarly writers.

The nucleus of a canon was quickly in evidence. Obviously letters which could show apostolic authorship were to be included, and also very soon the four gospels, to the exclusion of all other similar attempts to tell the story of the Lord's life. But there was for long a kind of fringe of uncertainty which included books which now form part of our Bible, and with them others which were gradually excluded. It will be useful to look at some of the evidence which has come down as to the way in which opinion varied in the second and third centuries.

In the second century most of the epistles contained in our New Testament are quoted, though 2 Peter, 2 and 3 John, and Jude are neglected. Just after the century divides we have Tatian's *Diatessaron*, a harmony of the gospels based on the four now accepted. A little later (*c.* 185) Irenaeus, whose testimony is especially valuable, since his early life was spent in Asia Minor and his later life in the West, regards the number of the gospels as almost part of the natural order, like the four quarters of the earth and the four winds. For such an idea to arise a comparatively long period of acceptance must be postulated.

At the end of the second century there is a very interesting document which probably originated in the Church of Rome, the Muratorian Canon, so called from the name of its discoverer in 1740. It accepts our four gospels (Matthew, it might be explained, is not actually mentioned as the beginning is missing), the Acts, fourteen Pauline epistles, Jude, two epistles of John, the Revelation of John, and also that of Peter, though with some reservation. There is no mention of Hebrews, 1 and 2 Peter, James, and one epistle of St. John. Irenaeus also fails to quote from James, 2 Peter, Jude, and 3 John. About the same time Clement of Alexandria omits these books, with the exception of Jude; but as a kind of compensation he adds certain writings which ultimately failed to get into the canon—the *Preaching of Peter*, the *Shepherd* of Hermas; whilst he regards Clement of Rome and the epistle of Barnabas as apostolic.

Turning to the West we find much the same attitude towards the canonical books in Tertullian. He fails to use James, 2 Peter, 2 and 3 John. In contrast with Clement of Alexandria he denounces the *Shepherd* which had definitely been declared to be non-Scriptural by synods in North Africa.

THE GROWTH OF DOGMA

The Syriac-speaking church of Mesopotamia, which lay rather outside the full stream of Christian life, had its own canon, to which it clung for some centuries. It used the gospels in the form of Tatian's *Diatessaron* (though the 'separate' gospels were not unknown), and accepted the Acts and the Pauline epistles.

At the opening of the fourth century the policy of the Roman government in the persecution under Diocletian forced the Church, and still more the individual Christian, to face the question as to what were and what were not sacred books. For this persecution made an especial 'drive' against the Christian Scriptures, rightly concluding that if these could be destroyed the whole movement would collapse. The Church held it lawful to hand over writings which might be valued so long as they were not inspired; the latter must be preserved at all costs. But even after the end of this last outburst no complete certainty had been attained; some volumes still hovered on the fringe of the canon, as readers of Eusebius will remember from his somewhat elaborate division of the claimants into three classes; those which were universally accepted, those which were still in dispute, and those which were rejected.

The first to insist that our present collection of New Testament books should alone be regarded as canonical was St. Athanasius in his Festal Letter for 367. His decision carried the agreement of the West; but in the East there were still churches which preferred their own conclusions, and in particular the Syriac-speaking churches.

That the matter of the canon came up so early for discussion was a great advantage to the life of the Church and the purity of its doctrine. It is true that no decision was made until quite late; but the question was one upon which the vigilance of Christians had been aroused, and if there was uncertainty as to the exact status of many writings, it was impossible for any new productions, however venerable they might claim to be, to gain admission. Had the question of the Canon been delayed until after Constantine it is quite conceivable that many comparatively worthless productions, owing to their having been read and valued by certain churches for a considerable time, might have been included in the New Testament. Local patriotism would have forced them on the Church as a whole.

CHAPTER VII

The Church's Achievement

THIS final chapter, as it is the culminating point of our study by position, so also is it in development. It will therefore in part be a summing-up of much that has gone before.

The achievement of primitive Christianity can only be gauged when the nature and diversity of the problems which it had to solve have been fully understood. They were four in number. In the first place it had to adjust its relations with the Mother Community from which it broke away—the Jewish people and religion. This adjustment was never successfully made, in fact there was no possibility of adjustment when once the Church realised that it had a world-wide mission, and Gentiles began increasingly to take their place in its ranks. Separation was the only solution and with it a growing enmity.

Secondly, the Church had to improvise an organisation fitted to the circumstances and needs of the diverse races which made it up. Such an organisation had to be strong enough to preserve unity, and yet supple enough to meet the strain that would come upon it. In this the Church had only partial success, for in its long history national and racial ambitions were destined not seldom to lead to schism and disruption.

Thirdly, the Church had to make its message comprehensible and acceptable to the Hellenic civilisation into which it pressed, and at the same time to preserve its own ethos. This task would have seemed to the contemporaries of the apostles, had they been aware of the existence of those who undertook it, to be one of complete absurdity. That a small band of Palestinian Jews should seek to divert the stream of civilisation and progress in order to irrigate tracts of their own chosing was ludicrous indeed.

Last of all the Church had to make good its position in a tolerant, yet at the same time, somewhat rigid political system; it had to settle its relation to the Empire. This, as we know, really involved a life-and-death struggle. The Church's acceptance of the challenge contained in this situation would have seemed equally absurd to the Roman citizen of the first century of the Christian era. Yet in spite of being drawn for the most part from classes which were despised and uninfluential, in spite of being under suspicion of disloyalty, in the end the Church overcame the Empire; or at least succeeded in imposing its own terms of recognition. In doing so it " swept before it the vested interests, prejudices, traditions and authority of the most powerful social and political organisation that the world hitherto had known ". (James Moffatt, in Harnack, *Expansion of Christianity*, p. vi.) It is to the closing stage of the struggle between the Church and the Empire that we must turn our attention before going on to discuss more general considerations.

THE CHURCH'S ACHIEVEMENT 143

The final struggle took place, or rather began, under Diocletian. This emperor, whose father and mother were both slaves, made it a matter of definite policy to exalt and magnify his office. He did so in the hope of bringing new life and order to a weakened and disorganised realm. Like Augustus, the founder of the Empire, he preferred to attain his ends by peaceful means wherever possible, but unlike Augustus and his immediate successors he was no longer bound by the traditions of the Republic; he could make naked despotism the policy of the ruler of the State. Hence his court had little to distinguish it from that of an Oriental monarch. The traditions of the Republic, however, had not died out entirely; they lived on still in the Senate at Rome.

One reason for the elevation of the office of emperor was a desire to increase his dignity; in addition it was also hoped that the isolation in which he now lived would ward off attacks of assassins such as had often brought disaster and civil war in the past. A further measure intended to guard against attempted revolts was the division of the Empire into two parts, each ruled by an Augustus, under whom was a Caesar. Thus if a rebel succeeded in overcoming one ruler there would still be three others to be conquered before his position could be considered secure. This knowledge would act as a deterrent to any future aspirant to power. For greater convenience of administration, and probably in order to get free of the neighbourhood of the Senate, Diocletian removed the headquarters of government from Rome, thus reducing that body to little more than an interesting survival. He himself took the East as his sphere, fixing his capital at Nicomedia in the north-eastern corner of Asia Minor. The capital of Maximian, the Augustus of the West, was at Milan.

In view of the peaceful nature of Diocletian and the fact that members of his family and suite were avowed Christians, it is a little surprising that after having reigned more than eighteen years he should suddenly authorise a new persecution. There can be but little doubt that he was persuaded to adopt this course by Galerius, the Caesar who helped him to govern the East, who was a determined opponent of Christianity.

On February 23, 303, the Pretorian Guards gave the signal for the outbreak by destroying the principal church in Nicomedia. The next day the first edict was issued. It ordered the demolition of all Church buildings and the burning of all Christian writings. Those who persisted in their faith were declared incapable of holding property; if officials they were to be deprived of their rank, and in certain cases were reduced to slavery. A supplementary edict in the following March ordered the arrest of all clergy. In December, however, a further edict granted them release on condition of sacrificing. Those who proved obstinate were to be tortured; a strange means of inducing acceptance of what was intended to be an amnesty.

Soon afterwards Diocletian became temporarily insane and Maximian issued a further edict in their

THE CHURCH'S ACHIEVEMENT

joint names by which all Christians were ordered to offer sacrifice or be liable to the extreme penalty. This was a distinct change of policy, and it would hardly have been accepted by Diocletian. His method had been to avoid bloodshed and the multiplication of martyrs, for this would only stiffen the Christian resistance and lead to fanatical outbreaks. Maximian's junior colleague in the West, the Caesar Constantius, was of a mild and humane disposition and he satisfied his conscience by pulling down a few churches and then ignoring the rest of the edicts. It is, however, probable that St. Alban was put to death at this time.

In May 305 the two Augusti resigned their offices and went into retirement. They were succeeded, in accordance with the scheme prepared by Diocletian, by the two Caesars, Galerius in the East and Constantius in the West. The accession of the latter meant that persecution in the West was now at an end. In the East, however, it became even more bitter when Galerius appointed his nephew, Maximin Daza, as Caesar. Six years later Galerius at last gave way. He was dying of a terrible disease and had come to see that Christianity could not be stamped out. Accordingly on April 30, 311, he isued an edict of toleration giving to the Church the right to carry on its own worship. Daza still continued to persecute after his uncle's death and put out a further edict by which civic authorities were ordered to expel all Christians from their cities. He tried to organise a great Pagan Church on lines similar to those of the Church to act as its rival, and very much on the lines of a modern dictator he made use of the educational system to enforce his special views. But his time was short, for being defeated by Licinius, the ally of Constantine, he fled to Tarsus where in August 313 he died of *delirium tremens*. In the previous March Constantine and Licinius had issued the Edict of Milan which gave liberty of worship to the Empire and so freed the Church from all fear of persecution or interference. In reality, since Constantine thereupon took it under his protection, it amounted to a virtual establishment of Christianity though actual establishment had to wait for the reign of Theodosius II at the end of the century. The action of Constantine was so momentous that we must now turn back to look at his career and the circumstances which led him, so far as they can be ascertained or surmised, to perform it.

Constantine was the son of Constantius and Helena, a woman probably of low rank, but evidently a legal wife and not a mere concubine as many state, since she had had to be divorced before Constantius, by the order of Diocletian, could marry the stepdaughter of Maximian. Constantine was brought up at the court of Diocletian and Galerius at Nicomedia, and there in all probability, rather than in the West, he acquired his impressions of the power of Christianity. After a time he joined his father, and on the death of the latter the legions at York, without consulting the reigning emperors, immediately proclaimed him Augustus. A series of brilliant military campaigns followed until the crowning triumph at the Milvian Bridge in 312 made him supreme in the West. Thereupon, as we have seen, he issued jointly with his brother-in-law, Licinius, the famous Edict of Milan.

Into the question of Constantine's religious motives, if any, we cannot enter. It is an unprofitable subject which can never really be decided one way or the other. But the political reasons which led him to recognise the Church as a valuable ally are plain and a tribute to the Church's importance and power.

The triumph of the Church was inevitable, even if Constantine had not seen this some other sooner or later would have done so, and the continuance of persecution would only have led to catastrophe. In many places the people and their magistrates, even though they were not themselves Christians, recognised the merits of the latter and objected strongly to the harrying of good neighbours and fellow-citizens. The truth of the matter was that the Church was alive and the Empire moribund; one was facing the past, the other stretching eager hands to the future. The Empire was no longer capable of 'creation', soon, in spite of the alliance with the Church, it would be unable even to maintain the measure of life which it then possessed. In the meantime there was need for some religious influence to bind the Empire together; the worship of the emperor had obviously failed to do this, the only alternative was to try the Gospel. Thus Constantine worked Christianity into the main pattern of the Empire's development.

What proportion the Christians bore to the rest of the inhabitants of the Empire at the beginning of the fourth century it is quite impossible to estimate. One thing may be taken as certain, the proportion differed very considerably in different parts, in the East it was without doubt very much higher than in the West. There were, however, Christians everywhere, not only in each several province of the Empire itself but out beyond its borders in the forests of Germany and the highlands of Persia. Furthermore, Christianity was stronger by far in the towns and great centres of population than in the scattered country districts. This would give to it an appearance of power greater than in reality it possessed. But in few places can its followers have approached even an equality in numbers with the pagans.[1]

Why, it may now be asked, and the question is of supreme importance, did the Church come to occupy this position of power and influence? What were the reasons for its triumph? The answers are, of course, many and various and cover a wide field of achievement and seized opportunity.

First in order may be placed the favourable situation of which the primitive Christians took such splendid advantage. Jesus Christ was born into the world in ' the fulness of the time ' (Gal. iv. 4); when the three great peoples of the ancient Mediterranean world, who met in the inscription over the Cross of Calvary

[1] The question has been examined in detail by Harnack, *Expansion of Christianity* ii, pp. 147–446.

(John xix. 20), had completed their work of preparation.[1]

The Romans, by establishing a single empire, had obliterated sundering national boundaries; to this empire they had brought peace and social stability, and strung along its great roads they had planted a number of cities, each a kind of model of the imperial city itself. As for the Greeks, they, after partially hellenising the East through the exploits of Alexander the Great, had in the West conquered with their culture the strong nation which had reduced them to political subjection. In doing so they had brought it about that a single language was understood by all persons of culture throughout the world, and using that language as a medium they had made men familiar with all manner of new ideas and problems. The Jews, for their part, had made a superb contribution in the sphere of religion, and had, moreover, provided in all the great cities of the Empire meeting-places from which the Gospel could make its first efforts in each locality to bring men, both Jews and Gentiles, to the knowledge of the Christ.

The Roman peace made possible the circulation of ideas and the movement of men. The roads were always full of hurrying travellers, traders, tourists, with wandering teachers among them, as well as the more solid mass of the legions. The Christian missionary was not slow to join these others and to find in the flow of international traffic the means of reaching his

[1] See further the late Bishop Talbot's essay in *Lux Mundi*.

journey's end, and the opportunity of evangelising on the way.

So ideas, religious, social and philosophical, travelled from one end of the Empire to the other, with the government looking on with tolerance, so long as no political unsettlement or grave moral offence was involved in their propagation. The problem of the Christian, with his obstinate refusal to conform to the official Emperor-worship, in the end proved too much for it; but time had been allowed, before any real or widespread attempt at suppression was made, for the Gospel to make itself secure in all parts of the Roman world. Then it was too late. The very worship of the emperors helped the Gospel, for it accustomed men to a religion which claimed to be universal, or at least limited by no national boundaries. So, too, the flood of Oriental religions which had invaded the West might give Christianity rivals for a time; but their failure to provide for the deepest needs of men sharpened spiritual hunger and made the truth more acceptable when at length it came their way.

Philosophy was never a serious rival, even among the educated; for thought under the Empire had reached a stage when it was given up too wholly to criticism. The traditional religions having been rejected, as indeed philosophers had always rejected them, reason was seen at length to provide no really satisfactory substitute. Negations called for something affirmative. Stoicism and Neo-Platonism, with its strange alliance of the philosopher and the adherent of the

THE CHURCH'S ACHIEVEMENT

old religious system, were but stop-gaps; it was in Christianity alone that final satisfaction could be obtained.

This brings us to the further question as to what it was in the message of the Church and in the characteristics of primitive Christianity which gave it the ability to meet the needs, not only of philosophers but of men and women in general. Why did they become Christians?

Again the answers are varied. The motives of some were clearly not of the highest, especially when the triumph of the Church was well in sight. Constantine might see in the Church a means for binding the Empire together; lesser men found in it a way to personal advancement. Others may have come in merely to get that fellowship and certainty which the world outside could not afford. Among causes more worthy, in the highest sense, there is again much variety, and those which our fathers ranked high in the list may prove to be less potent than they imagined. This is certainly true of the Christian claim to be able to work miracles, a subject which may well be cleared out of the way at the outset.

The ability to work miracles was not regarded as of high evidential value by the contemporaries of the early Christians, for the very simple reason that it was too common. The time was one of superstition and credulity and the agent of every religious propaganda was expected to provide miracles, just as in the Middle Ages it was a poorly equipped monastery or church which could not produce, perhaps a wonder-working relic, but at any rate a relic of some kind or another. So miracles were by no means impressive. The opponents of Christianity did not deny the truth of their miracles —Celsus, for example, accepted those of the gospels— but they would have agreed with the Christian apologists that such powers were no evidence of divine power or favour, the demons could work miracles just as readily. Each party to the dispute would regard its own works of power as valid, but condemn those of its opponent as deceitful and devilish.

So, too, in regard to martyrs. The effect of their witness depended very largely on the presuppositions of the spectators or hearers, and also on the behaviour of the actual victims. Justin, himself to end his life as a martyr, was moved to the study of Christianity by the constancy and courage of those who gave up their lives for the faith; but to Marcus Aurelius, a man of high mind and great ideals, they were simply obstinate and ignorant men whose conduct and motives he failed utterly to comprehend.

Some of the martyrs undoubtedly behaved in an extraordinary way, and their deaths, provoked by acts of violence and sacrilege, were clear cases of suicide. They were mere vulgar fanatics, such as are found in all religions, whose inspiring motive was bravado rather than real faith. In later times martyrs of this type became a distinct embarrassment, not only to the magistrate but to the Church, and, indeed, the title was at length denied to those who deliberately sought death in this manner. To die for the faith was not quite so simple a matter as it might seem; "one requires genius, even for martyrdom", as Goethe makes one of his characters say. The act of Cyprian in going into hiding during persecution, because his life was of value to his people, shows more of real Christian character than the passionate desire of Ignatius to be offered up at Rome and his fear that the Roman Christians might at the last prevent it. It was not necessarily the highest type of character which went to the stake, and those who survived their witness, the so-called confessors, often proved difficult to the Church's officials by reason of their pride and self-assertion. A less highly organised society might indeed have given them greater scope.

The comprehensive organisation of the Church was, however, without any doubt one of the reasons for its victory. The conversion of individuals might take place through personal influence, wives bringing in their husbands, and slaves their masters and mistresses, but for solid advance a firm organisation was demanded. This, as we have already seen, the Church succeeded in hammering out under the pressure of grave needs within and without. Under its system the separate communities were bound together and a sense of their common fortunes aroused. Travellers from one church to another went to and fro in a continual stream, and to Rome most of them came sooner or later as to the centre of the whole Church and Empire. Literature also was circulated and exchanged, and events in one church were communicated to others by means of letters. There were, of course, gaps in the system here and there, and much ignorance of the fate of obscure communities. Melito of Sardis, for example, writing before the last quarter of the second century, is quite unaware of the persecutions in the adjacent province of Bithynia which took place in the first quarter of the same century.

Co-operation between the churches was matched, in a manner which made a strong appeal to pagans, by a real sense of brotherhood between individual Christians. The Jews and the votaries of Isis and Mithras made a free use of the term 'brethren', and tried to make it a reality; but with the Christians it had a deeper meaning, and the fellowship to be found within a congregation was stronger than that in any heathen guild. Pachomius, the famous monastic pioneer, who served in the army of Constantine, is said to have become a Christian because of the attitude of Christian soldiers towards one another. It was a truly valuable characteristic, and one can readily imagine groups of Christians, of different races and even of different tongues, drawn together in some foreign city and in face of common danger; barriers of habit and custom would be broken down, comradeship would count for more than race, and a new sense of brotherhood would arise with the realisation that the one great thing they had in common was of more significance than the many things in which they differed. A striking manifestation of fellowship was the exercise of a lavish hospitality; a virtue which Clement of Rome actually places on a level with faith itself. Another manifestation was the care of the sick and old, especially in times of plague and panic; this care was even extended to pagans and created an immense impression.[1]

The extent to which the victory of Christianity can be attributed to intellectual factors is uncertain. Probably such factors made it easier for those without to give it a hearing, especially if they were of a philosophical cast of mind, and removed obstacles. The work of the apologists must have helped to make the Gospel more 'respectable' in the eyes of the learned, and the School of Alexandria doubtless did much for the furtherance of the Gospel. Benefit to the Church may also have come with the exposure of the failings and absurdities of Polytheism. This, however, had been done over and over again by heathen philosophers, and the Christian attack revealed nothing very new. The higher minds must always have found themselves faced by the pertinent question:

"Can men worship
Souls as little godlike as their own?"

But the continuation of the attack was necessary when Paganism showed signs of revival, and so became worthy of the use of satire, a weapon which is not commonly wasted on systems which are dead and harmless. For some the appeal to prophecy, that is to the Old Testament, was of value; Tatian says that

[1] There were some striking instances during the great plague at Alexandria (c. 259): see Eusebius vii, 22 and cf. also ix, 8.

" certain barbarian writings " brought him knowledge and help which the philosophers had failed to afford. It was not Jews alone who would be impressed by this line of argument, but heathen as well, for it would show them that the Church's pedigree was longer than they had supposed. It claimed, in fact, to go back to the Creation.

From the first the Church, following the Lord's example, had taught 'with authority'. Its members had shared in a great experience, continually renewed, and, like the blind man in the fourth gospel (John ix. 25), they were supremely confident of one thing, even if they were unable or unwilling to explain it. Bare assertion, when based on a first-hand experience, is very impressive to a certain type of mind; and there were many minds in that age, as in our own, who were open to such impressions. Some of these, craving for certainty, no doubt accepted Christianity almost in a spirit of despair, as a way of escape, as the only probable solution of the mysteries and problems of existence. Particularly would they be attracted by its claim to provide a mediator through whom God, who was regarded as transcendent and entirely separate from man, could be approached and known. On another plane the Gospel message satisfied longings which had been aroused by the Mystery Religions for a Saviour, and satisfied them, not with some mythical hero, but with a historical person. The gospel of Redemption was indeed good news for those who were perplexed and defeated by the ills of soul and body alike.

The enthusiasm of the first mission preachers of the Gospel, although it might arouse the scorn of the educated, was another factor which must have counted for much with the common people. For the Christians had a message, at once profound and simple, which had thrilled their own souls. Men and women of no importance in the eyes of society, they were so obviously conscious of boundless horizons, and something of the freshness of the early world seemed to radiate from them, for their message was one which concerned a Living God.

That the Gospel message had power to change lives and to raise up even the most degraded was evident from almost countless instances; but not all were thus affected, and the problem of convincing converts who had been brought up as heathen that religion and morals were closely connected was a vast one. Indeed, one might say that it constituted at one and the same time the Church's hardest task and its greatest opportunity for manifesting the power of the Gospel. To take such people and transform them into something to which the title 'saint' could be applied, however inappropriately, was a supreme achievement. Converts from Judaism had already a high moral standard, as need hardly be stated; but those from Paganism, unless they had belonged to some philosophical school, required long training and instruction before they were fit for baptism. Even then there were many failures. Hermas, to give an example, reveals the low state of many Roman Christians in the first half of the second century; the clergy themselves were not above reproach, and alongside proud, worldly and self-seeking presbyters he refers to dishonest deacons. But, in spite of failures, the average Christian was notably more moral and more honest than his heathen neighbour. Justin, indeed, could claim that a frequent cause of conversion was the impression made by the honesty of Christian business-men upon their pagan customers.

When Gibbon, in the famous fifteenth chapter of *The Decline and Fall of the Roman Empire*, tried to discover reasons to account for the spread of Christianity much was hidden from him, both of the religious conditions of the Roman world and of the methods of the Church, which has been recovered in the century and a half since he wrote. Gibbon was also a little handicapped by the necessity of conciliating orthodox opinion—an occasional jibe alone tells us that his tongue was often in his cheek. A writer of the present day has thus a much greater knowledge than was possible for Gibbon, and, even when he writes from a Christian point of view, is no longer compelled by a regard for traditional opinions to conceal the truth as he sees it. It can now be admitted freely that one secret of the Church's growth is to be found in the extraordinary power of adaptation which it exhibited. Paganism was largely conquered by being absorbed, and much of it reappeared in a Christian guise. In this the Church showed itself to be more accommodating than Judaism before it. To Judaism there was always something suspect and dangerous about the

Greek spirit. A measure of adaptation might be possible in the Dispersion, and in remote districts conformity to foreign ideas was probably much greater than was at one time supposed, unless the cult of Sabazios in Phrygia was quite an isolated instance. The wide and versatile spirit which animated the Church and enabled it to absorb and include all manner of diverse beliefs and customs was one of the characteristics which manifested its capacity to be a universal religion. No religion which insisted on preserving its own narrow series of doctrines and ritual could ever have hoped to fulfil such a destiny in the Greco-Roman world of the first few centuries of the Christian era.

The process of adaptation began early; in fact, it may be said without serious exaggeration, that the Church came under Hellenistic influences from its very birth. If it was a sect of Judaism, as is often asserted, it was a sect of Liberal Judaism, and indeed partly a sect because of its liberalism. Among its first missionaries were men of wide outlook who had already some sympathy with Hellenic ideas; and in St. Paul, of Tarsus and Jerusalem, an ideal instrument was at hand to speed the process on its way. It was, by a strange coincidence, in Ionia, the western fringe of Asia Minor where European philosophy had had its birth, that the task of intellectual adjustment was seriously taken in hand. St. Paul's captivity epistles were written to Ionia (or even in Ionia if Professor Duncan's hypothesis of an Ephesian captivity is correct), and it was quite natural that St. Peter, in writing to the same neighbourhood, should refer to the necessity for "giving a reason for the hope that was in them" (1 Peter iii. 15). Above all it was in Ephesus that the fourth gospel was composed, a writing which the late Canon Streeter declared to be " the boldest ' restatement ' of Christianity in terms of contemporary thought ever attempted in the history of the Church ". (*The Four Gospels*, p. 468.)

As converts from heathenism pressed in they would bring with them not only a low moral standard which required constant watching, but also an outlook on life that was definitely sub-Christian. In spite of careful training many of them failed to throw off these earlier influences, and in time the Church itself was slowly affected by them. Sometimes their influence was seen to be evil and excluded as heresy; more often its effect was so gradual that Christianity itself was sufficiently modified to be able to receive it. The Church, moreover, in appealing to heathen would naturally tend to emphasise those aspects of its teaching and practice which would be calculated to attract them. The process of modification by incorporating elements from the life and thought around was highly dangerous for the very reason that it was so largely unconscious; furthermore, it was often due, not to the deliberate action of the learned and godly, but to the sheer pressure of popular demand. This latter circumstance was, of course, almost a commonplace of the Middle Ages, when many doubtful beliefs and practices were thrust upon the Church, almost against its will; but it was not lacking even in the earlier years.

Paganism, for its part, was also modified by contact with Christianity; it has indeed been stated that by the beginning of the fourth century their theology was much the same, since both believed in a supreme God; where they differed was in their mythology, since they gave different names to that God and His satellites. This statement is an exaggeration so obvious as hardly to be misleading; but it contains a good deal of truth; was, indeed, to become even more true of later centuries. Syncretism was in the air and there can be no reasonable doubt that the Church proved much too hospitable to notions that were really incompatible with the Gospel. When their true nature was realised the task of excluding them was one of excessive difficulty, and the eventual process of purgation was never sufficiently drastic or sustained.

Such pagan accretions, however, were not entirely evil; for God had not left even pagans without some witness of Himself. Myths and legends appeal to the imagination and may be said to have a representative value; they convey truths to simple souls which historical events often fail to make real. The thought and culture of the age was not merely a snare, it had a lesson to teach those who were possessed of sufficient spiritual insight to know what to receive and what to reject. " While Christianity, with its Trinity of divine Persons, its God-made man, its pantheon of divinised men and women, is open to the superficial charge of being a reversion to the pagan polytheistic type, it is rather to be regarded as taking up into a higher synthesis those advantages of polytheism which had to be sacrificed for the greater advantage of a too abstract and soul-starving monotheism." Such is the opinion of Father Tyrrell (*Lex Orandi*, p. 148). The same may be said of the pomp and magnificence of the heathen tradition of splendid ceremonial which was taken over by the Church when full liberty of worship became possible and the acquisition of suitable buildings. This, with other pagan conceptions, was baptised into the service of Christ, but like many another forcible conversion, it was unaccompanied by any change of heart. The ritual might still remain pagan in essence, even though applied to Christian conceptions.[1]

Thus the triumph of the Church was bought at a price, and if it gained much it had also its losses. The same is true of the connexion with the State which Constantine's action was to bring about.

Constantine still kept the title of *Pontifex Maximus*, as did his successors for more than a generation. He was thus head of both the Christian Church and official Paganism; and his attitude towards each of them was practically identical. As emperor he was supreme in religion as in other matters. The Church was to be controlled by him just as much as the State, and it may

---

[1] It is perhaps worth pointing out that Hellenism had just achieved a similar triumph over Indian religious thought. Hinduism, in its earliest form (i.e. in the days of the Vedas), knew of no worship of idols; this, so A. J. Toynbee suggests, came in with Greek influences: see *A Study of History*, i, p. 87.

be said that the Church, in that age at least, was quite willing that so it should be. The imperial patronage, thus accepted and acknowledged, was bound to lead to all kinds of worldly temptations, to the pursuit of influence by political means, and to the increase of luxury and self-seeking. The Church and its ministers would also be drawn into the political sphere, with its dark intrigues and tortuous methods. All this would involve a loss of spiritual power, for which material gains were but a sorry compensation. Moreover, the close identification of the Church and the Empire and its peculiar civilisation would prove a stumbling-block to Eastern Christians. Many of the heresies of Egypt and Syria had a national complexion and were a kind of protest against this identification. Christianity had long ceased to be a Semitic religion when the wave of Islam broke over the Empire; the Arab conquest in the East, and even in parts of the West, was facilitated by the desire of some types of Christians to be free from the rule of a joint Empire and Church which they regarded as lacking in sympathy with their peculiar aspirations.

So long as the Church was separated from the world it was strong to influence the world; its very intolerance, based as it was on ethical grounds, must have given it attractive power in the eyes of some of the best of the heathen. With the coming of power came the spirit of compromise. Even the cessation of persecution had its loss as well as its gain, for constant danger had secured sincerity and increased the sense of brotherhood. Popularity and imperial favour, on the other hand, led to an ungodly rush of pagans into the society which held the future. As in some mass movement areas in the present-day mission field, the Church must have been embarrassed by its success, and found it difficult, if not impossible, to cope with the numbers desiring entry. Thus there must have been a vast increase of merely nominal and conventional Christianity. Constantine's patronage as Dante saw (*Inferno* xix, 115), gave birth to much evil for the Church, even though the Donation was not actual fact.

Constantine demanded in his new instrument unity and a fixed standard of belief. Henceforth synods and councils were to pass decrees and canons enforceable by the State, which would be binding on all those concerned. The loss of freedom, partial only it is true, was the price paid for position and power. So, too, imperial patronage would make permanent the difference between clergy and laity, for it gave to the former the privileges and immunities enjoyed by heathen priesthoods. The endowments, which now became theirs, also exempted them from the necessity of following secular callings.

But if the adoption of the Church by Constantine led the way to much that was evil, it gave to the Church a great opportunity for the promotion and fostering of all that was good. It was henceforward free to develop in all directions, so long as it did not attempt to cross the imperial will. The task of making the Empire Christian in all its activities was laid upon

THE CHURCH'S ACHIEVEMENT

it. The first fruits of the Church's influence can be seen in the legislation for which Constantine was responsible with its many humanitarian provisions, a continuation and extension of the work of the Stoic lawyers of the age of the Antonines. Women and children, slaves and criminals, were all to receive greater consideration and more merciful treatment. If the exposure of children, in spite of the Church's condemnation, was not made a crime, it was discouraged. Public opinion was not yet ripe for it, and the futility of going in advance of public opinion was seen in the non-observance of the law forbidding gladiatorial shows. It needed the heroic sacrifice of the monk Telemachus to bring them to an end nearly a century later.

Justice is a relative term, and we can no more devise laws which will be valid for all time, than set up a standard of art to serve as a model for every subsequent age; but it can hardly be denied that the provisions were an expression of the new Christian character of Constantine's rule. Other proceedings were perhaps not so happy, for the Church, released from persecution itself, speedily took in hand the task of suppressing Paganism and persecuting heresy. At first there was no actual prohibition of pagan worship unless the rites were immoral or too bloody; but many temples were destroyed or plundered, and the way was shown for more stringent treatment in future reigns. But this was not a grave injustice, for the meagre survivals of Paganism had really no right to retain such magnificent buildings. That Paganism was dead was seen in the absence of any desire for martyrdom on the part of its advocates.

To the Empire itself the alliance with the Church must have brought fresh life and energy enabling it to realise ideals and ambitions which had hitherto proved elusive. This was well brought out by Sir William Ramsay in an article in the *Expositor* for December 1889, where he wrote: " One of the most remarkable sides of the history of Rome is the growth of ideas which found their realisation and completion in the Christian Empire. Universal citizenship, universal equality, universal religion, a universal Church, all were ideas which the Empire was slowly working out, but which it could not realise till it merged itself in Christianity." Unfortunately the Empire by this time was too exhausted, economically and physically, for it to prove capable of meeting the ever renewed thrusts of the barbarian peoples beyond the frontiers. But if the Church did not prevent the fall of the Roman Empire it succeeded in salving much that was precious from its civilisation and in handing it on to those who were its conquerors. This was no light achievement in itself.

So the curtain comes down at last; but again may it be repeated, the drama is not ended—a drama which has an end is, after all, only a romance—it merely marks the close of a scene or, at most, an act. The drama of the Church's life is age-long, its contest with sin and falsehood, with lust and greed, still goes on, in the world around and in the heart of each one of us. We cannot be content to be mere spectators, we are compelled by the example of those who have gone before if by nothing else to play our parts in making actual the Church's ideal, in bringing nearer the day when the kingdoms of the world shall become the Kingdoms of the Lord and of His Christ.

INDEX

A

Acilius, Glabrio, 60
Agapé, the, 117, 118
Alban, St., 145
Alexander the Great, 22, 29, 149
Alexander Severus, Emperor, 66 f.
Alexandria, 27, 33, 129; Church of, 46, 91, 93, 103, 113, 129 ff., 155
Antioch, 37 f., 46 f., 71, 85, 113, 136
Antoninus Pius, Emperor, 63, 73
Apocryphal writings, 78, 89 f.
Apollonius, Martyr, 65
Apollonius of Tyana, 67
Apologists, the, 57, 72 ff., 93, 128, 152, 155
Apostolic Constitutions, the, 120
Aristides, Apology of, 73
Arles, Council of, 98, 113
Arnold, Matthew, 155
Artemon, 85
Asceticism, 80 f., 88 f.
Associations, 20, 55, 104 f., 117
Athanasius, St., 139
Athens, 17, 73, 129
Augustine, St., 98, 120
Augustus, Emperor, 13, 23, 29, 143
Aurelian, Emperor, 71

B

Baptism, 118 f., 134
Bardesanes, 91
Barnabas, St., 38 f.
Barnabas, Epistle of, 47 f., 138
Basilides, 90 f.
Bithynia, 55, 61, 119, 154
Blandina, Martyr, 12, 64
Britain, 21
Burkitt, F. C., 111

C

Caecilian, Bishop, 98
Canon (New Testament), 81, 94 f., 119, 135–140
Caracalla, Emperor, 66
Carpocrates, 91
Carthage, 69, 71, 97, 98, 113, 132
Catacombs, the, 60, 70, 119
Celsus, 75, 90, 104, 152
Cerinthus, 84
Cities, 14, 21, 32, 148, 149
Claudius, Emperor, 53
Clement of Alexandria, 129 f., 138
Clement of Rome, St., 47 f., 136
Clement, Epistle of, 47 f., 57, 105, 107, 137, 155
Clergy, the, 105 ff., 116, 144, 158, 164
Collingwood, R. G., 21
Commodus, Emperor, 64 f.
Constantine, Emperor, 34, 98, 116, 146 f., 151, 162 ff.
Constantius, Emperor, 145 f.
Cornelius, Bishop, 97
Corinth, 47, 105, 107, 117
Creeds, 133–135
Creighton, Bishop Mandell, 116
Cynics, the, 28
Cyprian, St., 69–71, 97, 107, 112, 132 f., 153

D

Damascus, 37, 103
Dante, 164
Davey, Noel, 121
Decius, Emperor, 68 f.,
Demons, 24, 74
Diatessaron—see Tatian
Didaché, 47, 103, 106

Diocletian, Emperor, 139, 143–146
Dionysius of Alexander, Bishop, 96, 124
Docetism, 88, 126
Domitian, Emperor, 60 f., 74
Donatists, the, 97 f.
Druids, the, 29, 53
Duncan, G. S., 159

E

EBIONITES, the, 83
Elagabalus, Emperor, 66
Eleutherus, Bishop, 96
Emperor, worship of, 24, 29, 55 f., 74 f., 112, 147, 150
Ephesus, 39, 58, 137, 160
Episcopate, the, 47, 49, 69, 71, 81, 99, 105–110, 119 f.
Eschatology, 43, 45 f., 56, 61, 82, 86 f., 95, 122
Eucharist, the, 58, 81, 108, 118–120, 135
Eusebius, Bishop, 46, 49, 50, 64, 67, 73, 139, 155

F

FLAVIA DOMITILLA, 60
Flavius Clemens, 60
Fronto, 64, 75

G

GALERIUS, Emperor, 144 f.
Gallienus, Emperor, 71, 109
Gardner-Smith, P., 118
Gibbon, Edward, 25, 65, 67, 68, 158
Glover, T. R., 22
Gnosticism, 84, 86–93, 96, 98 f., 111, 123, 125
Goethe, 15, 153
Gwatkin, H. M., 95, 110

H

HADRIAN, Emperor, 44, 62, 73
Harnack, A. von, 39, 104, 108, 148
Hebrews, Gospel according to the, 84
Helena, Empress, 34, 146

Hellenism, 21 f., 42 f., 126 ff., 149, 158 ff.
Henderson, B. W., 14
Heresy, 36, 77 ff., 98 f., 124 ff., 137
Hermas, 48, 110, 124, 138, 157 f.
Herod Agrippa, 41, 43
Holy Spirit, the, 35, 36, 86, 95 f., 111, 116, 124, 131 f.
Hort, F. J. A., 108
Hoskyns, Sir Edwyn, 121

I

IGNATIUS, St., 46, 49 f., 77, 109, 114, 153; Epistles of, 49, 136
Irenaeus, St., 50, 91, 93, 128 f., 137 f.

J

JAMES, St., 41, 114
Jerome, St. 34
Jerusalem, 33 ff., 43 f., 102, 113, 114, 159
Jewish Christianity, 39, 41–43, 54, 84, 104, 122
Jews, the, Judaism, 30, 32 ff., 53, 56, 59, 121 f., 149, 154, 158 f.
John, Acts of, 92
John, St., 36, 39
John the Elder, 39, 50
Josephus, 43, 72
Julia Mamaea, 66
Julius Africanus, 124
Julius Caesar, 20, 132
Justin Martyr, St., 12, 43, 64, 87, 92 f., 120, 123, 128, 152, 158
Juvenal, 114

L

LICINIUS, Emperor, 146 f.
Lightfoot, Bishop J. B., 15, 49, 63 f.
Loewe, H., 119
Lyons, 64

M

MAJORINUS, 98
Marcia, 65
Marcion, 93 f.
Marcus Aurelius, Emperor, 63 f, 65, 152

INDEX

Martyrs, 53, 64 f., 69, 145, 152 f.
Maximian, Emperor, 144–146
Maximilla, 96
Maximin, Emperor, 67
Maximin Daza, Emperor, 145 f.
Melito of Sardis, 33, 154
Mensurius, Bishop, 98
Milan, 144, Edict of, 146 f.
Mill, J. S., 64
Minucius Felix, 64, 75, 124
Minucius Fundanus, 62 f.
Miracles, 76, 151 f.
Mithras, 27, 154
Moffatt, James, 142
Monarchianism, 84 ff., 125 f.,
Montanism, 85, 95 f., 111, 116, 132
Muratorian canon, 138
Mystery religions, The, 26 f., 156

N

NEO-PLATONISM, 27, 150 f.
Nero, Emperor, 13, 55, 57, 59 f., 74
Nicomedia, 144, 146
Noetus, 85
Novatianism, 97, 107
Novatus, 97

O

OCTAVIUS, the—*see* Minucius Felix
Oriental religions, 24 f., 29, 53, 150
Origen, 48, 66, 75, 130–132

P

PACHOMIUS, 154
Paganism, 19 f., 31, 73, 145 f., 157 f., 161, 165 f.
Palestine, 33, 75, 104
Pantaenus, 129
Papias, 46, 50 f.
Patripassianism, 85, 96
Paul, St., 36 ff., 54, 60, 70, 99, 102 f., 110, 115, 121, 159
Paul and Thecla, Acts of, 111
Paul of Samosata, 71, 85
Pella, 42
Penance, 48 f., 110 f.

Persecutions, 24, 52 ff., 139, 142–147, 150, 154
Peter, St., 35 ff., 60, 70, 114 f., 160
Peter, Preaching of, 39, 138
Philip, Emperor, 67 f.
Philip, St., 36
Philo, 33, 72, 129
Phrygia, 25, 95, 159
Pistis Sophia, 111
Plato, 27, 63, 131
Pliny the Younger, 16, 61 f.
Plotinus, 27
Polycarp, Bishop, 46, 49 f., 63, 136
Pompey, 14, 26
Pothinus, Bishop, 64
Praxeas, 85, 96
Priscilla, 96
Prophets, Christian, 47, 82, 96, 106

Q

QUINTILIAN, 17

R

RAMSAY, Sir William, 56, 166
Rashdall, Hastings, 122 f., 125
Roman Empire, the, 12 ff., 74, 142, 147, 149, 166
Rome, 59, 62, 67, 68, 92, 102, 144; Church of, 46, 47 f., 71, 103, 113–115, 136, 138, 153, 157 f.
Rostovtzeff, M., 14

S

SABAZIOS, 159
Sabellius, 85 f., 126
Samaria, 36, 87, 92
Scriptures, the, 43, 76, 99, 118 f., 131, 135, 139, 155 f.
Septimius Severus, Emperor, 66
Shepherd, the—*see* Hermas
Simon Magus, 36, 87
Smyrna, 46, 60, 111
Socrates, 28, 124
Sohm, Rudolf, 12
Stephen, St., 35 f., 42
Stoicism, 27, 128, 150, 165
Streeter, B. H., 92, 128, 160
Symeon, Bishop, 62